Algebra and the Elementary Classroom

Transforming Thinking, Transforming Practice

Maria L. Blanton

Foreword by Megan Loef Franke

HEINEMANN
Portsmouth, NH

Heinemann
361 Hanover Street
Portsmouth, NH 03801–3912
www.heinemann.com

Offices and agents throughout the world

The author and publisher wish to thank those who have generously given permission to reprint borrowed material:

Figure 2.6 and Appendix: "The Candy Problem" from *Algebra and the Early Grades* edited by James J. Kaput, David W. Carraher, and Maria L. Blanton. Copyright © 2008. Published by Lawrence Erlbaum Associates, Inc. Permission conveyed through Copyright Clearance Center, Inc.

"T-Shirt Problem," Figure 3.6 and Appendix: "Trapeziod Table Problem," and Figure 4.2 and Appendix: "Handshake Problem," adapted from "Developing Elementary Teachers' Algebra Eyes and Ears" by Maria L. Blanton and James J. Kaput in *Teaching Children Mathematics*, October 2003, Vol. 10, Issue 2. Copyright © 2003 by the National Council of Teachers of Mathematics. Reprinted with permission from the National Council of Teachers of Mathematics. Permission conveyed through Copyright Clearance Center, Inc.

Figure 3.13 and Appendix: "Squares and Vertices" adapted from "From Matching to Mapping: Connecting English and Mathematics" by Sitsofe Enyoman Anku in *Mathematics Teaching in Middle School*. Copyright © 1997 by the National Council of Teachers of Mathematics. Reprinted with permission from the National Council of Teachers of Mathematics. Permission conveyed through Copyright Clearance Center, Inc.

Library of Congress Cataloging-in-Publication Data
Blanton, Maria L.
  Algebra and the elementary classroom : transforming thinking,
transforming practice / Maria L. Blanton ; foreword by Megan Loef Franke.
     p. cm.
  Includes bibliographical references and index.
  ISBN-13: 978-0-325-00946-9
  ISBN-10: 0-325-00946-5
  1. Algebra—Study and teaching (Elementary). I. Title.
  QA159.B53 2008
  372.7—dc22   2007044103

Editor: Victoria Merecki
Production service: DB Publishing Services, Inc.
Production coordinator: Sonja S. Chapman
Cover design: Jenny Jensen Greenleaf
Compositor: Aptara, Inc.
Manufacturing: Steve Bernier

Printed in the United States of America on acid-free paper
12 11 10 09 08 VP 1 2 3 4 5

My initial forays into algebraic thinking as a teacher were unforgettable and not at all what I expected. I was teaching a second-/third-grade combination class. The students were experienced at solving problems using strategies that made sense to them, describing their strategies and listening to their classmates share their strategies. I felt comfortable with my abilities as a teacher of mathematics. I paid attention to students' mathematical thinking, drew on research-based knowledge to make sense of what I heard from students, and pressed students to make sense of mathematics. So, the idea of engaging in algebraic thinking was exciting. I saw that my students were already engaged in some algebraic thinking, I just needed to do more. I was prepared. Or so I thought.

My surprise came as I opened up opportunities for what Blanton discusses as *generalized arithmetic* by posing a true/false number sentence (see Chapter 2). My students jumped in with abandon. Seriously. I seeded one conversation around the identity of zero and they wanted to talk about commutativity of addition and then commutativity of multiplication. They wanted to talk about adding zero to a number and taking zero from a number. They wanted to talk about odd and even. They raised so many different ideas that I had no idea how to respond. I just wrote what they said all over the board. I thought they would have trouble talking about the ideas and that, at the most, I could push them to talk about the conjecture around zero I wanted the students to talk about. Instead, there were so many potential conjectures to pursue, I got stuck. I thought: How do I decide which one to pursue? How do I follow all the different mathematical ideas students raise? How do I make sure students hear the different ideas and make sense of them? I was thrown into an amazing mathematical tangle that I needed to get a handle on if I was going to be helpful to my students.

Algebra and the Elementary Classroom provides support for navigating all the questions I had for myself. Blanton establishes how capable students are of algebraic thinking; she warns that students can surprise us. She provides details that help teachers know what to listen for, and she provides a rich and relevant description of the mathematics. I had an idea of a task from my arithmetic work that might stimulate conversation around algebraic thinking, but I was not sure what to listen or look for in my student responses. I had not yet developed what Blanton calls "algebra eyes and ears." She describes in detail how to navigate the conversations around conjectures and students' algebraic thinking. She carefully characterizes the conceptual and practical understandings teachers need to support student learning.

As a researcher, I have had the opportunity to learn from teachers as they engage in supporting students' development of algebraic thinking in elementary school. I have learned from their practice about what it takes to support the development of students' algebraic thinking. The questions teachers ask, the ways they follow up on student responses and then support students to detail their thinking can make a difference in students' articulating their algebraic ideas and can make a difference in what they learn. Along with my colleagues, I have found, for instance, that when teachers ask a sustained series of probing questions as a follow-up to students' thinking, students have more opportunity to make explicit the details of their ideas for themselves and others in the class. However, when a teacher asks a "bundle" of questions to follow up on student thinking-meaning, a series of questions with little pause and no response in between-students rarely articulate their thinking further.[1] Our research suggests time and time again that pursuing student thinking in ways that press students to articulate, relate their ideas to others, keep track of those ideas, and talk to others about them is related to the development of mathematical understanding and the development of their algebraic thinking.

Blanton argues that good questions are the foundation of supporting algebraic thinking. In Chapter 6 she states, "One of the most important

---

[1]Franke, M., N. Webb, A. Chan, M. Ing, D. Freund, & D. Battey. (2007). "Eliciting student thinking in elementary school mathematics classrooms." Paper presented at the annual meeting of the American Educational Research Association. Chicago, Il.

things you can do to develop children's algebraic thinking is ask good questions. . . . Asking good questions gives *children* the opportunity to organize their thinking and build mathematical ideas." She goes on in this chapter, and throughout her classroom examples, to articulate the specific questions teachers can ask to support the development of students' algebraic thinking. She embeds the kinds of questions one would ask in the work of listening to students, representing their thinking, and supporting generalization. Attending to the details of *Algebra and the Elementary Classroom* provides the support we need as teachers to embed the development of students' algebraic thinking in our teaching of elementary school.

Reading Blanton's *Algebra and the Elementary Classroom* provided me, an experienced teacher, with new ideas about tasks to draw upon, additional details about student thinking, and a wider range of questions to ask. Had I read it before my initial forays into algebraic thinking, I would not have been as surprised about my students' responses, and I would have had ideas about what to listen for and what would have been productive to accomplish mathematically.

Megan Loef Franke
UCLA

This book was originally planned as a collaboration with Jim Kaput. It represents the culmination of our work in local schools, and it is deeply imprinted with his thinking about and passion for making important ideas of mathematics, particularly algebra, accessible to children, teachers, and even school administrators. Jim was not only a national leader in rethinking the ways we view the teaching and learning of algebra, he was also a fixture in local schools as we worked to understand how to make algebra relevant to elementary school teachers and their students. I am greatly indebted to him for his contributions to this book. It is poignant that his untimely death prevented him from seeing its completion.

I would like to acknowledge the teachers whose ideas and classroom experiences are included here. Their insights are an essential piece of this work. But while their contributions are visible, there are many other teachers whose particular work is not represented here, but whose role in the preparation of this book has been extensive. All of these teachers transformed their classrooms into laboratories, their private teaching practices into public forums, so that we could flesh out the conceptual ideas of algebra in the elementary classroom. They were creative, open, and enthusiastic. They taught *us*.

Much of the work on which this book was based was supported by a grant from the U.S. Department of Education Office of Educational Research and Improvement to the National Center for Research in Mathematics and Science Education and, subsequently, the National Center for the Improvement of Student Learning and Achievement based at the

University of Wisconsin Center for Research in Education. Support for the exploration of new ways of thinking about mathematics in the elementary grades has been—and is—critical.

I would like to thank Heinemann editor Victoria Merecki for her support in initiating this project and for her assistance as it was completed. The expertise she brought to this process was extremely valuable. I am also grateful for the reactions and advice given by the reviewers, and I would like to especially thank Linda Levi. Her experience with teaching children mathematics for understanding led to particularly insightful comments. Finally, I would like to thank those teachers who read earlier drafts of this book and offered both suggestions and encouragement for making the ideas presented here accessible to their peers.

What, today, is the *really* important mathematics that young children should learn? The NCTM *Principles and Standards for School Mathematics* (2000) answers this question with a road map of content and processes to guide teaching in the elementary grades. One of the main features of this road map is algebra, or algebraic thinking.

The *Principles and Standards for School Mathematics* views algebra as a strand of content that begins in pre-kindergarten and extends through grade twelve. But in practical terms, what do elementary classrooms that "do" algebraic thinking look like? What is the role of the teacher? What is expected of students? What does the curriculum look like? This book is designed to help answer these (and other) questions about elementary classrooms that develop children's algebraic thinking. While based on a number of years of research, it is intended to take a practical, teacher-oriented approach. It draws on elementary teachers' classroom-tested materials, children's work, classroom vignettes, and teacher reflections to illustrate:

1. how teachers can tap into the algebraic potential of their own resources and materials and transform these into opportunities for algebraic thinking;

2. how algebraic thinking supports children's basic arithmetic skills;

3. how teachers can transform their classroom practice so that algebraic thinking becomes a part of children's daily experience in viable ways;

4. how algebraic thinking can be integrated into other subject areas; and

5. how algebraic thinking can become a part of school culture.

Start with Your Own Resources

It is important to understand that *algebraic thinking is not an add-on to your curriculum*. That is, it is not a set of concepts or skills you teach after you've done the "real" work prescribed by the curriculum in place. Instead, it is a way of thinking that permeates all mathematics and is the heart of what children should be doing routinely in school mathematics.

Tasks that support algebraic thinking can be generated directly from the materials you have at hand, so there is no need for "add-on" materials to compete with your own curriculum. Nor do you need to wait for your school to get the perfect curriculum. Many of the activities you use with your students can be transformed in simple ways to bring out underlying mathematical properties and structure that support algebraic thinking.

> Many topics that I cover as part of my curriculum are embedded in algebraic thinking tasks. Therefore, [these tasks] do not have to be considered an add-on, but can be thought of as an extension of what we already do.
>
> *Laura Hunt,*[1] *third-grade teacher*

So, *start with your own resources*. You have a wealth of possibilities right at your fingertips. As a first step, look at what you plan to teach in your next lesson and consider the question, How can I get students to think about what is going on mathematically *in general*? Throughout this book, you will find techniques that answer this question, and over time, you will develop your own "algebra eyes and ears" and find that noticing ways to bring algebra into your daily instruction will become second nature to you.

> [After doing only two algebraic thinking activities], I had a new outlook on math. I knew that I wanted to integrate algebraic thinking into every topic I did. The truth was that our curriculum was wonderful. It allowed plenty of ways to integrate this way of thinking. I just hadn't noticed up to this point. I want to add algebraic thinking problems

---

[1]Teachers' names are their real names.

throughout the program. I now realize that this can be done. You don't have to be given problems. You can develop your own.

Angela Gardiner, third-grade teacher

Overview

This book is based largely on a multiyear research and professional development project. While the ideas discussed here were developed in a broad spectrum of classroom demographics, the primary setting was an urban school district. But regardless of the classrooms, schools, or districts in which this work occurred, the common denominator has been a cadre of creative, dedicated elementary school teachers—many of whose ideas and experiences are contained in the pages of this book—who have used their classrooms as laboratories for rethinking their own knowledge of mathematics and teaching. *Their* work, and that of teachers like them, has helped us better understand teaching algebra in the elementary grades.

The book is divided into four sections. It begins by looking at the nature of algebraic thinking and its place in the elementary grades (Section I, "The Nature of Algebraic Thinking"), then shifts to an exploration of the content of algebraic thinking and how it fits into the curriculum (Section II, "Changing *What* I Teach"), teaching practices that support students' algebraic thinking (Section III, "Changing *How* I Teach"), and novel ways to integrate algebraic thinking outside of math classrooms (Section IV, "Changing *Where* I Teach").

Section I discusses the nature of algebraic thinking in the elementary grades—both what it is and what it is not—and places it within the context of school reform in mathematics education.

Section II focuses on the mathematical piece of the story. It explains particular aspects of algebra content for the elementary grades and how you can transform your own curriculum resources into opportunities for building, expressing, and justifying mathematical relationships. It examines how to transform arithmetic concepts that you currently teach and how to introduce new and important concepts about functions and patterns that will prepare students for mathematics in later grades. It also illustrates how children can build—not lose—arithmetic skills through algebraic thinking.

Section III focuses on teaching practices that develop children's algebraic thinking. Tasks alone are not sufficient in teaching your students to think algebraically. How you implement these tasks is equally important. This section looks at important skills such as questioning strategies teachers might use to build algebraic thinking, listening to students' ideas in order to mine opportunities for algebraic thinking, helping children represent their ideas in multiple ways, helping children identify mathematical relationships, and so on. Teachers' classroom vignettes are used to illustrate these ideas.

Finally, Section IV addresses a practical concern for teachers faced with many demands on their classroom time. It looks outside of the math classroom—across different subject areas and through various school activities—to identify creative ways to make algebraic thinking a more visible part of children's daily school experience. It provides lessons and activities, developed and tested by teachers, to make connections among mathematics, language arts, social studies, science, and even physical education. It also discusses teachers' ideas for how to build a school culture that encourages children to think algebraically.

Throughout this book you will find action items titled Teacher Task or Think About It. Their purpose is to develop your understanding of important ideas about algebra and how you teach it. Teacher Task items provide opportunities to solve algebraic thinking problems, design tasks appropriate to the grade you teach, and explore how you might introduce particular concepts to your students. Think About It items have similar components, but their focus is to reflect on your mathematical experiences and knowledge, as well as your own teaching practice.

You will find many algebraic thinking tasks throughout this book. As you encounter each one, take time to solve the task before continuing. Working through the concepts on your own will prepare your thinking for the narrative following each task. As an additional help, solutions for many of these tasks are included in Appendix A. Solutions for selected Teacher Task and Think About It items are found in Appendix B and Appendix C, respectively. Keep in mind that the solutions given here offer one way to think about the task. Depending on the grade level you teach, your students might give solutions in different forms or reason about the task in different ways. They might express their answers in words rather than symbols. The solutions here are a guide for your own thinking, but consider how your students might represent their own ideas and be prepared for other possible strategies they might offer.

As you read through this book, it is important not to lose sight of the most crucial participant in building an algebraic thinking classroom—you! The ideas of algebraic thinking endorsed in national and state frameworks, new curriculum materials, teacher professional development programs—even this book—will remain hidden to children unless elementary teachers engage them in the daily work of thinking algebraically, of building, expressing, and justifying mathematical relationships. The goal of this book is to provide you with the necessary tools to do this.

The Nature of Algebraic Thinking

If I had to explain what is algebra to a student, I would say, "Think of all that you know about mathematics. Algebra is about making it richer, more connected, more general, and more explicit."

—Ricardo Nemirovsky, as quoted in Erick Smith

How would *you* explain algebra to your students? What is its purpose? This section introduces what we mean—and don't mean—by algebra in the elementary classroom. It begins a story, developed throughout this book, about how algebra can make mathematics "richer, more connected, more general, and more explicit" and, by doing so, can transform it into an unexpected adventure for your students.

CHAPTER 1

What Is Algebraic Thinking?

People often think of algebra as manipulating letters or symbols to solve complicated equations or to simplify algebraic expressions (NCTM 2000). But algebra—and algebraic thinking—goes much deeper than that.

The heart of algebraic thinking is building, expressing, and justifying mathematical relationships, or generalizations (Kaput 2008). Broadly speaking, in mathematics a *generalization* is a statement that describes a general truth about a set of (mathematical) data. For example, the statement "The sum of an even number and an odd number is always odd" is a mathematical generalization because it captures a true relationship in a set of data (here, the data are integers). It characterizes what happens when you add *any* even number and *any* odd number. Generalizations can be expressed in different forms. Children might initially express the generalizations they observe in words (for example, "Any time you add zero to a number, you get the same number back"). Over time, as their mathematical language matures, they can learn to express these ideas in more symbolic ways (for example, "$a + 0 = a$, where a is any real[1] number").

---

[1]This property is true for a class of numbers called *real* numbers, although your students might understand the property to be true for, say, natural numbers because that is the domain of numbers they understand. Most of the numbers you and your students encounter in elementary grades will be natural numbers (0, 1, 2, 3, . . .), fractions, or integers. These numbers are all real numbers. The set of real numbers consists of two types of numbers: rational numbers and irrational numbers. A rational number is one that can be expressed as the quotient of two integers, where the denominator is not zero. Rational numbers include the natural numbers, since any natural number can be expressed as itself divided by one. For example, 3 can be expressed as $\frac{3}{1}$. Note that 0 can be expressed as $\frac{0}{1}$. (How else can 0 be expressed as a quotient of two integers? Why?) Similarly, integers, which are defined as any positive or negative whole number or zero, are also rational. On the other hand, irrational numbers are those real numbers that are not rational. A well-known

This book explores what it looks like for children in elementary classrooms to build, express, and justify generalizations—to think algebraically—and how your teaching practice can support this. As a starting point, let's look at different aspects of algebraic thinking.

Different Aspects of Algebraic Thinking

Algebraic thinking comes in different shapes and sizes. The *Principles and Standards for School Mathematics* Algebra Standard states that children in the elementary grades should be able to

1. Understand patterns, relations, and functions;

2. Represent and analyze mathematical situations and structures using algebraic symbols;

3. Use mathematical models to represent and understand quantitative relationships; and

4. Analyze change in various contexts. (NCTM 2000, 37)

To help build a picture of what these learning goals look like in the elementary classroom, this book focuses on two key areas of algebraic thinking: (1) using arithmetic to develop and express generalizations (generalized arithmetic) and (2) identifying numerical and geometric patterns to describe functional relationships (functional thinking). While algebraic thinking contains other mathematical domains (Kaput 2008), generalized arithmetic and functional thinking form the focus of much of the current research on children's algebraic thinking (see, e.g., Kaput, Carraher, and Blanton 2008) and will provide us with a comprehensive starting point.

Generalized Arithmetic

The basic ideas of algebra as generalized arithmetic should be anticipated by activities in the early elementary grades and learned by the end of middle school. (Kilpatrick, Swafford, and Findell 2001, 419)

---

example of an irrational number is the number π. Unlike rational numbers, irrational numbers cannot be expressed as the quotient of two integers. The conversations you have with your students about the tasks in this book will likely involve only rational numbers. As students' algebraic thinking develops, it is important for you to understand how these rational numbers are related to each other so that you and your students can explore the greatest set of numbers for which a conjecture holds true.

Generalized arithmetic refers to building generalizations about operations on and properties of numbers. Through this, children generalize important mathematical ideas such as commutativity, learn how operations affect numbers, and develop a relational view of equality. For example, as children experience adding, subtracting, multiplying and dividing numbers, they begin to notice certain regularities in how numbers behave. One type of regularity they observe is that the order in which two numbers are added does not matter. They learn to see and express this commutative property of addition initially using natural language ("You can add numbers in any order."). As children mature mathematically, they can learn to express this idea in more formal ways, using symbols[2] to represent any two numbers: The statement "$a + b = b + a$, for all real[3] numbers a, b" is a formal expression of this generalization.

Chapter 2 looks further at specific ways you can generalize the arithmetic concepts you currently teach. As a companion to this, Chapter 5 examines how algebraic thinking supports the development of children's arithmetic understanding, including the arithmetic skills and procedures that are a necessary part of thinking algebraically.

Functional Thinking

We believe that from the earliest grades of elementary school, students can be acquiring the rudiments of algebra, particularly its representational aspects and the notion of variable and function. (Kilpatrick, Swafford, and Findell 2001, 419)

Functional thinking draws on a different skill set than does generalized arithmetic. It requires children to attend to change and growth. It involves looking for patterns in how quantities vary in relation to each other. A *function* is a way to express that variation. Functional thinking also gives children opportunity to work with a rich set of tools—tables, graphs, functions machines, input/output charts, and so on.

As with generalized arithmetic, these relationships might be expressed using children's natural language or in more symbolic forms. For example,

---

[2]Throughout this book, the term *symbol* refers to the use of literals (letters) or nonliteral symbols (e.g., ◇) to represent unknown or varying quantities.
[3]Since this property holds for real numbers, it also holds for subsets of real numbers. You can adapt the set of numbers being used based on the age of your students. For example, your students might explore the Commutative Property of Addition for whole numbers.

very young children might describe a relationship between the number of children in their classroom and the total number of hands as "the number of hands doubles" or "you add two every time." While these descriptions are rudimentary, they are an important starting point in being able to attend to how two quantities vary together. As children mature, they can learn to describe this relationship in symbols (for example, as $H = 2 \times C$, where H is the number of hands and C is the number of children).

Chapters 3 and 4 look more closely at understanding and expressing functions, classroom examples of children's thinking about functions, and developing functional thinking tasks from the materials you have on hand.

What Algebraic Thinking Is *Not*

We have just considered what algebraic thinking is. It is also important to know what it is *not*. Algebraic thinking in the elementary grades, or *early algebra*[4] as it is sometimes called, is not traditional high school algebra (as you likely experienced it!) repackaged for young children. As described earlier, people sometimes think of high school algebra as learning rote procedures for manipulating symbols and solving equations (NCTM 2000)—in short, a symbol-driven marathon of factoring, simplifying, and solving.[5]

THINK ABOUT IT 1.1

What do you think of when you hear the term *algebra*? What were your experiences with high school algebra?

Early algebra, instead, is designed to help children see and describe mathematical structure and relationships *for which they have constructed meaning*. Children construct meaning as they gather data, look for relationships in the data, develop and express conjectures[6] about these relationships, and build arguments to support their conjectures.

---

[4]The term *early algebra* is used in this book to refer to algebraic thinking in the elementary grades.

[5]In more recent years, however, high school algebra has also begun to change to reflect our growing insights into teaching mathematics for understanding.

[6]The term *conjecture* refers here to a mathematical claim or statement that is either true or false. We will explore this more throughout the book. See, in particular, Chapter 6.

This activity thrives in classrooms where children sift through each other's ideas and where teachers find ways to bring children's thinking into the center of learning. It is marked by mathematical explorations, investigations, and conversations. While children in elementary grades may develop some incidental skill at symbolic manipulation, the goal is instead that they learn to reason algebraically and that they begin to acquire a symbolic, "algebraic" language for expressing and justifying their ideas.

Starting Assumptions

Algebraic thinking empowers children. It is learnable: All children can learn to think algebraically. In fact, much of the work discussed in this book occurred in urban schools with diverse learners and in districts with economic and educational constraints.

> I had a great moment during class when one of my lowest students solved the problem and was so excited about what he had done. Not only did he solve it, he was the first to do so, and his math confidence has been sky high ever since.
>
> *Andrew Gentile, fourth-grade teacher*

> Children who had previously been reluctant math learners were suddenly engaged and energized by algebraic thinking activities. They worked with one another, developed argumentation skills, and communicated math in a multitude of ways. Their work in itself is proof that teaching elementary students algebraic concepts is viable. People who observed my students in action were amazed that they were third graders. We all felt a sense of empowerment.
>
> *Laura Hunt, third-grade teacher*

It is also teachable: Every teacher can build a classroom that develops children's algebraic thinking. As you read this book and test its ideas in your own classroom, keep these starting assumptions in mind:

1. The ability to make and defend generalizations is at the heart of mathematical power and can be learned by all children.

2. Children can deepen their understanding and skill with any particular mathematical topic by generalizing and building arguments for their generalizations.

3. In order for the mathematical power of generalizing to develop, the classroom environment must foster meaningful inquiry and communication.

4. Teachers must be able to find, extend, and exploit their instructional resources to serve their evolving needs.

5. Communities of teachers can learn from and teach each other, even when the ideas are new to everyone involved.

Throughout this book, we will explore in more detail what algebraic thinking looks like both in and out of the math classroom—the kinds of generalizations children might build, how they might express them, the types of arguments they might use to turn a strong intuition into a generalization, how you can create activities and design instruction to support this, and how you can find opportunities beyond your own math classroom to get children to think algebraically.

Changing *What* I Teach

We had been plugging away at these tasks for a few weeks and the excitement was building. When I wrote a new functional thinking task on the board, something different happened. Four students simply sat and scrutinized the blackboard. In the past, everyone would take out papers and begin to write. Two of the students said, "I know this!" within a matter of seconds. I was amazed at the quickness and accuracy of their thinking, and I knew at this point that these tasks were definitely paying off in my class.

—Andrew Gentile, fourth-grade teacher

Early algebra might be unfamiliar territory for you. This section looks closely at the content of early algebra and how you can transform your existing resources and materials into opportunities for algebraic thinking. It discusses ways to generalize the arithmetic you teach and to build children's functional thinking skills. It draws on teachers' classroom experiences to illustrate how you can build these mathematical ideas into your own practice, and it includes vignettes of children's thinking as evidence that they can think algebraically. The aim is to help you develop algebra "eyes and ears" so that you see the mathematics you currently teach in new ways, ways that will better prepare your students for the more complex mathematical thinking of the twenty-first century.

Generalizing Arithmetic
Finding Algebra in Arithmetic

The *Principles and Standards for School Mathematics* (NCTM 2000) is clear about the importance of developing students' algebraic thinking skills across grades pre-K through twelve, not just in high school. But if you are an elementary classroom teacher, how do you integrate algebraic thinking into your daily instruction? Perhaps your district has an older curriculum in place that has no apparent links to early algebra. Or, maybe it has a new curriculum with many innovative ideas, but not a strong connection to algebraic thinking. Where do you begin? Because arithmetic is likely a central part of your curriculum, this chapter examines how you can help your students think algebraically about important concepts in arithmetic.

Transforming Number and Operation

> Students who work with algebraic problems are well positioned to discover numerical concepts that are building blocks for future mathematical study. For example, there are many opportunities to discuss how the numbers 0 and 1 function in mathematical equations. If children are exposed to generalizations at an early stage, they will be better equipped to tackle the more abstract concepts that come later.
>
> *Laura Hunt, third-grade teacher*

There are many important arithmetic concepts for children to learn in elementary grades. But children should know more than how to execute

$$12 + 27 \qquad 30 + 15 \qquad 11 + 21$$

$$45 + 23 \qquad 16 + 14$$

Figure 2–1 *Adding two-digit numbers for computational practice*

arithmetic skills and procedures.[1] Algebraic thinking can bring a deeper purpose to arithmetic and children's arithmetic understanding.

THINK ABOUT IT 2.1

What percentage of your math lesson focuses on learning arithmetic skills and procedures? What percentage focuses on generalizing arithmetic?

Generalizing arithmetic includes helping children see, describe, and justify patterns and regularities in operations on and properties of numbers. Although children might use this knowledge routinely—but implicitly—when they're doing arithmetic, algebraic thinking helps lift these properties out so that children are aware of them and can point to them as tangible objects of learning. In turn, this awareness reinforces their understanding of arithmetic concepts.

Arithmetic Is Not Just for Adding

Let's think about how arithmetic concepts might be extended to include algebraic thinking. In instruction that focuses on arithmetic, you might ask children to add a random set of two-digit numbers (see Figure 2–1) in order to develop computational skills. But if algebraic thinking is your goal, you

---

[1]While arithmetic understanding is broader than learning a set of skills or procedures (for example, children need a conceptual understanding of place value, not just procedural skills for adding whole numbers), learning skills and procedures can sometimes become a dominant part of arithmetic instruction.

$$12 \qquad 27 \qquad 45 \qquad 23$$
$$+\,27 \qquad +\,12 \qquad +\,23 \qquad +\,45$$

Figure 2–2 *Adding two-digit numbers to explore the Commutative Property of Addition*

can develop a set of sums that leads children toward an important generalization (and still gives them computational practice). Consider the set of sums given in Figure 2–2.

If you ask children to focus on their solutions in relation to the addends in these problems, they will notice that the order in which the numbers are added does not matter. For example, the result of $12 + 27$ is the same as that of $27 + 12$. Ask them to describe what they notice: It is important that children be given opportunities to write and talk about their ideas. They might pose a conjecture in their own words such as, "You can add numbers in any order."

If children use natural language to describe their conjecture, can you guide them toward a more symbolic way to express their ideas? For example, how could they represent "any number"? Would they use a letter? What does the letter symbolize or represent? How would they represent two different (arbitrary) numbers? Can they use the same symbol to denote both? Why or why not?[2]

With guidance, children can learn to express the property illustrated here (the Commutative Property of Addition) in a form such as $a + b = b + a$, where a and b represent any (real) numbers. Of course, you will need to keep in mind the age and experience of your students when transforming conjectures from natural language into symbolic form—but don't underestimate what they can do!

Finally, ask children to think about whether (or when) their conjecture is true. Does their conjecture always hold? For which numbers is it true? Or, for what types of numbers is it true? That is, does it hold for really big numbers or really small numbers? Does it hold for negative numbers?

---

[2]As a matter of mathematical convention, we use different symbols when referring to (potentially) different numbers. For example, we would express the Commutative Property of Multiplication as $a \times b = b \times a$, using a and b to denote two possibly different numbers. Note that the property also holds if the numbers happen to be the same (for example, $3 \times 3 = 3 \times 3$).

How do they know? How would they convince someone else their conjecture is true? (See Chapter 6 for a more detailed treatment of testing conjectures and the forms of justifications children might use.)

Through this activity of analyzing, conjecturing, justifying, and (for some children) symbolizing, children move beyond arithmetic to algebraic thinking. But it can start with a simple set of tasks (Figure 2–2) whose arithmetic purpose has been retooled to lift out the algebra in the arithmetic.

> **(?)**
>
> **THINK ABOUT IT 2.2**
>
> What other operations are commutative? That is, do numbers commute under subtraction, multiplication, or division? Depending on your grade level, develop a set of practice exercises to help your students explore these ideas. (See Appendix C, page 196, for an explanation.)

Generalizing the Commutative Property of Addition is a task that can be easily adapted to most grade levels. In fact, you might already be doing this type of activity in your class. It is included here to emphasize the point that generalizing arithmetic does not have to be very different from what you already do. By an easy transformation, an exercise for practicing addition skills can be extended to a powerful opportunity for developing, expressing, and justifying a mathematical generalization about operations on numbers. You only need to look at the arithmetic you already teach with "algebra eyes" so that you can structure arithmetic lessons around the broader goal to build algebraic thinking.

Children can notice and describe many arithmetic properties, such as "zero plus any number is zero" (Additive Identity Property), or "you can multiply two numbers in any order" (Commutative Property of Multiplication), or "if you subtract a number from itself you get zero" (Additive Inverse Property). Figure 2–3 lists some properties—or generalizations— that are important in understanding arithmetic.

> **TEACHER TASK 2.1**
>
> For each of the properties in Figure 2–3, develop a sequence of arithmetic tasks that would help children generalize that property. How do children express and justify their generalization? How can you help them express their generalization in a more symbolic form?

Arithmetic Property	Natural Language Expression	Symbolic Expression*
Commutative Property of Addition	"You can add two numbers in any order."	$a + b = b + a$
Commutative Property of Multiplication	"You can multiply two numbers in any order."	$a \times b = b \times a$
Associative Property of Addition	"If you're adding three numbers, you can add the first two, then the last, or you can add the last two, then the first."	$(a + b) + c = a + (b + c)$
Associative Property of Multiplication	"If you're multiplying three numbers, you can multiply the first two, then the last, or you can multiply the last two, then the first."	$(a \times b) \times c = a \times (b \times c)$
Additive Identity	"Anytime you add zero to a number, you get that number back."	$a + 0 = a$
Additive Inverse	"If you subtract a number from itself, you get zero."	$a - a = 0$
Multiplicative Identity	"Anytime you multiply a number by one, you get that number back."	$a \times 1 = a$

Figure 2–3 *Important generalizations in arithmetic*

*While *a*, *b*, and *c* represent any real numbers, children can explore these properties for the number systems that are familiar to them (e.g., counting numbers, whole numbers, integers, and so on).

Properties of Evens and Odds

While some generalizations in arithmetic are important enough to be named (like those in Figure 2–3), there are many other ways to generalize arithmetic. For example, operations on even numbers and odd numbers can lead to a rich source of algebraic thinking. You can easily organize computations on evens and odds so that children can practice arithmetic skills and procedures as part of the bigger goal of learning to think algebraically.

As with the Commutative Property of Addition illustrated earlier, building algebraic thinking into operations on evens and odds can be easily introduced into the arithmetic you already teach. For example, if whole-number addition is a skill your students are learning, design a set

	Sample Teacher Questions
12 + 18 =	What do you notice about the addends? (They're even.)
22 + 18 =	What do you notice about your solutions? (They're even.)
28 + 14 =	What can you conjecture about the sum of two even numbers? (An even number plus an even number will be even.)
34 + 26 =	Do you think this is always true? Why? For what numbers is it true?

Figure 2–4 *Addition exercises that can lead to generalizations about evens and odds*

of addition exercises that can be used as a springboard for thinking about properties of evens and odds (see Figure 2–4).

TEACHER TASK 2.2

Develop a set of multiplication problems that helps children think about what happens when they multiply any two odd numbers. Will the result be even or odd? Why? If your students haven't learned multiplication yet, use addition.

As an additional help, Figure 2–5 provides a set of questions you might use to help your students generalize about operations on evens and odds. (You will need to adapt these to your grade level.)

Fifth-grade teacher Laura Panell wrote about her students' thinking on adding evens and odds:

Marla[3] was the first one in the class to see the pattern. She came up to me and said, "I think I found out the answer to the last question."[4] "All right," I said. "Let's see what you did." She told me, "When you add two odd numbers together, you end up with an even answer, and

---

[3] All student names are pseudonyms, except for names crediting student poems.
[4] The question was, "What if you had some odd numbers but didn't know how many there were. If you added them together, what can you say about whether you would get an even number or an odd number for your result?"

Generalizing with Evens and Odds

■ What happens when you add an odd number and an even number? Is the result even or odd? Make a conjecture that shows what you found. How do you know your conjecture is true? Will it always work?

■ What happens when you add three odd numbers? Four odd numbers? Suppose I told you I was going to add a lot of odd numbers together but I didn't tell you how many. What could you say about whether my result would be odd or even? How do you know your conjecture is true? Will it always work?
(You can repeat these questions for even numbers.)

Extensions:

■ What happens if you change the operation to subtraction? Do the same results hold? (Note that this can involve negative numbers!)

■ What happens if you change the operation to multiplication? Do the same results hold?

Figure 2–5 *Generalizing with evens and odds*

when you add three odd numbers together, you end up with an odd number."

I looked around the room and everyone was in agreement with Marla's answer. I then wrote on the board:

$$1,895 + 1,987 + 2,073 + 5,999$$

I wanted to see if my class had made the generalization with this activity. Could they make the determination for larger numbers just as easily as they could for the smaller numbers? I then asked, "Without calculating these numbers, can anyone tell me if this set of numbers added together would end up being odd or even and why?" "Even," Gail said. "It is even because there are four numbers and that is an even amount of odd numbers so it's even."

I then asked if they would be willing to make this into a conjecture that we could all agree on. "Once we all agree on the wording, we will hang it up with our first conjecture from last week," I said. Travis raised his hand. He stated, "When you add an odd amount of odd numbers, you will get an odd number. When you add an even amount of odd numbers you will get an even number." I wrote this conjecture on the board.

Laura made an important choice in asking students *not* to compute 1,895 + 1,987 + 2,073 + 5,999. Her action required students to reason about the structure in the numbers. In particular, because all the addends were odd and there was an even number of (odd) addends, the sum would be even. To answer Laura's question ("Without calculating these numbers, can anyone tell me if this set of numbers added together would end up being odd or even and why?") without computing the sum, students had to know and apply a generalization about adding an even number of odds. Thus, instead of solving the problem arithmetically by computing the sum, students reasoned algebraically from the structure and properties of the numbers.

This represents an important progression in children's algebraic thinking. However, when children initially explored this question, they looked at specific cases to test what was happening with the sums. So, while there was a larger algebraic goal in this task, the exploration itself involved important computational practice for students. As Chapter 5 discusses more fully, not only can children find algebra in arithmetic, they can also find arithmetic in algebra!

Give students time to explore the questions in Figure 2–5 or a version modified to fit your grade level. Encourage them to make conjectures about their findings, to build arguments for whether their conjectures are true, and to discuss their findings with their peers. Finally, show your students how important their true conjectures (generalizations) are by putting them on display in your classroom.

Making a Known Quantity Unknown

Children are often asked to solve simple arithmetic word problems such as, "If Marta has $6 and Nathan has $3 more than Marta, how much money does Nathan have?" Children might use counters, play money, or their own drawings to represent the different amounts of money and construct a number sentence to solve the problem: $6 + $3 = $9 (the amount of money Nathan has). However, by removing information (such as the amount of money Marta has), you can transform this simple arithmetic task into one that uses algebraic thinking:

If Marta has some money in her bank and Nathan has $3 more than Marta, how much money does Nathan have?

The known amount that Marta had ($6) is now unknown.

Children cannot use arithmetic to solve this new problem. (In fact, the answer is not a numerical value.) Instead, they need to be able to represent the (unknown) amount of money that Marta has. This may seem awkward for children at first, especially if they have only worked with arithmetic tasks, known quantities, and solutions that are always a single numerical value. But after some experience, children recognize that they do not need to know how much money Marta has in order to describe how much Nathan has. They learn to accept the ambiguity of not having a specific numerical value to assign to the amount of money Marta has (and, thus, that Nathan has).

Ask your students questions that allow them to represent the unknown amount of money Marta has (don't tell them how to represent it). Questions such as "What do you know about the amount of money Marta has?" "How would you describe this amount?" "What do you want to call this amount?" and "Why?" can help children establish that the amount of money Marta has is unknown and think about ways to represent this.

You can then guide children to compare the amount of money Marta and Nathan have: How much money does Nathan have compared to Marta? Does he have more or less? What operation would you use to represent more money? Given your description of the amount of money Marta has, how would you describe the amount of money Nathan has in relation to that?

As you guide children's thinking, they can learn to symbolize the amount of money Nathan has as (for example) $m + \$3$, where m represents the amount of money Marta has. Younger children might express this in natural language as "The amount of money Marta has plus 3 more dollars." The use of symbols (or, in the case of younger children, natural language) to represent an unknown or varying amount is an important part of algebraic thinking. And when you introduce symbols in a natural way, allowing them to emerge in the context of problems that engage children's thinking, over time children will begin to use this "new" language to talk about their own mathematical ideas.

THINK ABOUT IT 2.3

Look at the arithmetic word problems you give your students. Is there a known quantity that you can make unknown? How might children solve this new task?

In a similar task, children across different elementary grades were asked to solve the following Candy Problem (see Appendix A, page 161 for a solution).

The Candy Problem

John and Mary each have a box of candies. Their boxes contain the same number of candies. Mary has 3 additional candies in her hand. How would you describe the amount of candy they each have? (Adapted from Carraher, Schliemann, and Schwartz 2008)

Not surprisingly, many children initially thought the problem could not be "solved" because the amount of candies in the boxes was unknown. To circumvent this, some children ignored the constraint about the unknown quantity and assigned a particular value to the number of candies in the boxes (e.g., John has 12 pieces of candy, so Mary has 12 + 3 = 15 pieces).

Some children constructed a table that allowed them to find a range of possible numerical answers for the amount of candies John and Mary had (see Figure 2–6). The use of a table suggests that children realized that the number of candy pieces in the boxes was unknown and could be any value, and they could not assign it a particular value. Their approach was to show that, while John could have different numbers of candy pieces, *if* he had a certain amount, then the number of pieces Mary had could be determined. Thus, while they were beginning to see that the number of John's candy pieces could be a range of values, they were not yet able to symbolize this idea.

Even so, children from different grades were able to express—and even symbolize—the amounts of candies that John and Mary each had. After a

John	Mary
5	8
6	9
7	10
8	11

Figure 2–6 *A table showing the corresponding numbers of candies John and Mary each had*

class discussion about the unknown number of candies John had, Julie Boardman asked her first-grade students to show in words or pictures the amounts of candies for John and for Mary. One child, Matt, drew two people. Underneath the first person (John) he wrote "some." Underneath the second person (Mary), he wrote, "some and 3." Matt's use of natural language to describe the amounts of candies was an important step toward symbolizing the unknowns in this task. He was able to accept the ambiguity of not having a specific numerical value for each amount and represent the unknown as "some." Older students were able to symbolize this idea. Fourth-grade teacher Andrew Gentile observed,

> The Candy Problem really helped the kids focus on symbolizing. I enjoyed watching the kids use pictures, letters, and even manipulatives to demonstrate that no matter what, Mary had $n + 3$ pieces of candy, where n represented the amount of candy John had. It was a real eye-opener for a lot of children who were struggling with the symbolic aspect of algebraic thinking.

Tasks like the Candy Problem offer an important way to use simple problems to help your students develop algebraic notation. Even in the early elementary grades (pre-K–2), children can begin to express unknown quantities using natural language as they did in Julie Boardman's first-grade class. Try the Candy Problem (or a task like it) with your students. Look at how they reason about the problem and whether (and how) they are able to represent unknowns.

Varying a Known Quantity

In addition to making a known quantity unknown, you can also vary a known quantity in a simple arithmetic word problem, transforming the problem into a series of tasks that allow students to build and test mathematical relationships. Consider the following simple arithmetic problem:

> I want to buy a tee shirt that costs $14. I have $8 saved already. How much more money do I need to earn to buy the shirt?

Children might solve this arithmetically using a variety of models that involve addition or subtraction. (In fact, you can use children's arithmetic models as a context for developing symbolic language. For example, an additive model could be expressed as $8 + A = 14$, while a subtractive model could be expressed as $14 - 8 = A$, where A [or some other symbol students select] represents the unknown amount of money.) They might represent their thinking with pictures, counters, play money, and so forth.

However, you can transform this task to an exploration of patterns and relationships by varying the cost of the item being purchased:

Suppose the tee shirt costs $15. If I have $8 saved already, write a number sentence that describes how much more money I need to buy the tee shirt. What if the shirt costs $16? $17? Write number sentences for each of these cases. If P stands for the price of any tee shirt I want to buy, write a number sentence using P that describes how much more money I need to buy the tee shirt. (Blanton and Kaput 2003)

Varying the cost of the tee shirt leads to a sequence of number sentences that might look like the following:

$14 - $8 = $6 (amount of money I need to earn)
$15 - $8 = $7 (amount of money I need to earn)
$16 - $8 = $8 (amount of money I need to earn)
$17 - $8 = $9 (amount of money I need to earn)

But the goal here is not just to solve the number sentences. Instead, it is to look at the set of sentences, identify what varies (the cost of the tee shirt), and use this to represent how much more money is needed for a tee shirt *of any price* (assuming the cost of the tee shirt is at least $8):

$P - 8$ dollars is the amount of money I need to earn.

Transformations like the tee shirt problem can be flexibly adapted to any arithmetic concept, such as multiplication or division, by simply varying one of the quantities. Mathematically, these types of tasks are much more powerful than solving a single number sentence. The "answer" is an expression ($P - 8$) for finding a solution to a broad class of problems, not just one. Like the task with Marta and Nathan, this task also requires students to understand that the solution might not be a numerical value. Developing expressions such as $P - 8$ or $m + 3$ gives children opportunity to symbolize their thinking while building their understanding of unknown or varying quantities as valid answers.

Algebraically, tasks like this help children think beyond the arithmetic—although this is the starting point—to describe a generalized quantity. And as children begin to think about and express unknown quantities or quantities that vary, they are being introduced to notions, such as *variable*[5] (see also Chapters 3 and 4), that are critical in the development of their mathematical thinking.

An Unequal View of =

One of the first symbols children encounter in school is likely =. But what meaning do they attach to this symbol? Ask your students to solve the following task:

$$9 + 3 = \square + 4$$

What number do you think they might place in the box? Why? Classroom studies show that children are most likely to add 9 and 3 and write 12 in the box. To many children, the symbol = means to compute the expression to its left and record the answer immediately after it (Carpenter, Franke, and Levi 2003). Certainly, teachers do not intentionally teach this view of equality. But, for example, the repetitive use of arithmetic tasks where children compute an expression then write their answer immediately after the = symbol can build a misconception in their thinking about what equality means. Many children fail to see the algebraic role of = as signaling a relationship between quantities, such as 9 + 3 is equivalent to, or *the same as*, $\square$ + 4.

It's easy (and important!) to help your students develop an algebraic view of equality. For some children, you might simply need to offer a set of tasks, like the one given here, and draw their attention to misconceptions in their thinking. An awareness of their thinking is a good starting point for developing an algebraic view of equality.

Alternatively, you can have children express their answers to computations as unexecuted operations, rather than as single-numerical-value answers. For example, instead of giving 37 as an answer to the sum 23 + 14, ask students to express their answer as the sum of two numbers. They might write 23 + 14 = 10 + 27, or 23 + 14 = 19 + 18. (In fact,

---

[5]*Variable* is used here to denote a letter or nonliteral symbol (such as $\triangle$) representing an unknown or varying quantity.

if a student suggests 23 + 14 = 14 + 23, you can build on this solution to talk about the Commutative Property of Addition.) This will help children see that the quantity to the right of the symbol = does not have to be a single numerical value.

Some teachers use a balance scale to help children visualize the idea of equivalent quantities. The scale allows children to work simultaneously with both sides of the equation (as opposed to operating only on one side, usually the left). June Soares described how one of her third-grade students learned to view equality after working with the balance scale.[6] She had asked students to solve the equation $(3 \times n) + 2 = 14$:

> Sam said that we could take the 2 away. He said that if we take the 2 from one side we have to take it from the other side. This was to make it balance. After we [took] the 2 away, he said to take the 12 tiles and put them in groups of 3. There were 4 groups, so the answer had to be 4. We tried replacing the *n* with 4 and it worked. (Blanton and Kaput 2005a)

Sam's reasoning required an algebraic view of equality; he did not know how to solve the problem by manipulating symbols in ways one might learn in a high school algebra course (i.e., subtract 2 from both sides, divide both sides by 3). Because he was able to see $(3 \times n) + 2$ and 14 (and later, $3 \times n$ and 12) as equivalent quantities, he was ultimately able to reason that the value of *n* was 4. Sam was able to see that quantities on either side of = were equivalent and that to maintain a balance, an operation on one quantity required the same operation on the second quantity.

Finding Missing Numbers

The discussion on equality pointed out how tasks such as 9 + 3 = □ + 4 can reveal the kind of understanding your students have of the symbol =. But as a missing number sentence, these tasks can also be a way to introduce literal symbols (as opposed to nonliteral symbols such as □) in your students' thinking.

As young children learn to use symbols, symbols become part of their language for solving problems. In June Soares' class, third graders began to

---

[6]Although the balance scale worked well in June Soares' class, this model might be problematic for your students (for example, it introduces issues of mass and distance from the fulcrum as factors in how the scale balances).

TEACHER TASK 2.3

Use the missing number sentence $9 + 3 = \square + 4$ as a simple way to introduce symbols to your students. Ask children what the symbol $\square$ represents. (They will sometimes say that $\square$ represents the "answer.") Ask if there is a more efficient way to describe this. (Children will sometimes say to represent $\square$ with A for the answer.) This can lead to the equation to $9 + 3 = A + 4$. While there is much more to do in the development of children's symbol sense, this might be a good place to start.

generate their own missing number sentences as a way to solve other problems. One example was the Triangle Puzzle (see Figure 2–7a), where a triangle is divided into regions with some of the regions containing numbers and others empty. The goal is to "complete the triangle" by finding all the missing numbers. The regions have additive relationships between them, and the missing numbers are determined by adding two side-by-side entries to determine the entry above them. For example, in Figure 2–7a, seven plus the unknown number to its right would be twelve, the entry above these two numbers. In solving this puzzle, Zolan generated a set of missing number sentences ($7 + a = 12$, $e + 4 = 5$, $4 + d = 7$) to solve for the missing numbers in the triangle. He first wrote and solved the number sentence

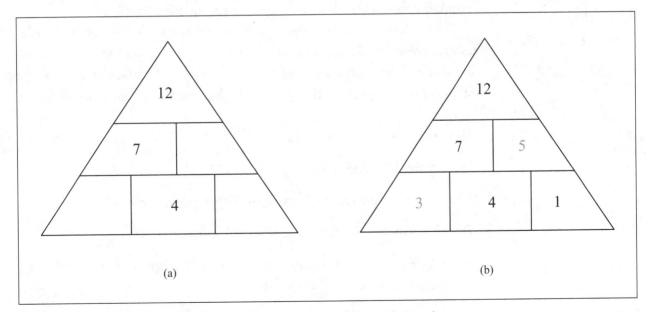

(a)

(b)

Figure 2–7 *(a) Triangle Puzzle and (b) Zolan's completed Triangle Puzzle*

$7 + a = 12$ to get $a = 5$, then used this to construct the sentence $e + 4 = 5$. The sentence $4 + d = 7$ could be solved without knowing other unknowns in the triangle. (See Figure 2–7b for Zolan's solution.)

Not only could Zolan symbolize unknown quantities, he understood that different symbols were needed for different unknown quantities. He was able to solve for the unknown in each equation and use that information in subsequent equations, finding that $a = 5$, $e = 1$ and $d = 3$. June had not asked students to use missing number sentences; for Zolan, this had become a way of thinking (Blanton and Kaput 2005a).

Stories about animals are a good source for tasks to help children symbolize and solve missing number sentences. You have probably seen problems like the following:

How Many Chickens?

Suppose Farmer Joe looks into his barn stall and counts 24 legs. He has 3 horses. If the remaining legs are on his prized chickens, how many chickens does he have? (See Appendix A, page 176, for a solution.)

There are a variety of ways children might solve this problem—some involving only arithmetic. For example, children might reason that 3 horses have 12 legs, so the chickens have to share the remaining 12 legs. Since each chicken has 2 legs, then there must be 6 chickens. To find this solution, they might draw horses and chickens and count out the legs, they might make 24 hatch marks to represent the total number of legs and group them in fours and twos (see Figure 2–8), or they might use a guessing method in conjunction with memorized number facts.

But you can also help children symbolize the unknown number of chickens and create a missing number sentence. Once children have determined that 3 horses account for 12 of the legs, a series of questions such as the following can help guide them to think algebraically about a solution:

"How many legs remain?" (12)

"How many legs does each chicken have?" (2)

"What information are we looking for?" (the number of chickens)

"Do we know the number of chickens?" (no)

"Since we don't know this, how do you want to represent or describe the (unknown) number of chickens?" (C)

"Can you use this information to write a multiplication sentence that helps us find the number of chickens?" ($2 \times C = 12$)

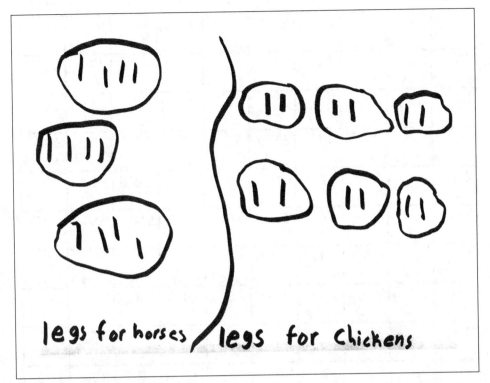

Figure 2–8 *An arithmetic model for finding the number of chickens, where the number of groups of two (6) represents the number of chickens*

"Based on your number sentence, what would the number of chickens, C, be?" (6)

While a student in secondary grades might manipulate the algebraic equation $2 \times C = 12$ by dividing both sides by 2 to solve for C, elementary children have different tools to help them solve this. For example, they might recognize a number fact (C = 6 because $2 \times 6 = 12$) or they might reason multiplicatively (if I add 2 six times, I get 12, so C = 6). (See also third grader Sam's reasoning about solving the equation $[3 \times n] + 2 = 14$.) The point of this task is that you can use it to help children think about representing unknown quantities and, by this, help them develop an algebraic language for solving tasks they might otherwise use arithmetic to solve.

Thinking Algebraically with the Hundred Chart

Opportunities for generalizing arithmetic are literally all around you! Do you have a Hundred Chart in your classroom? When June Soares' third graders were looking for patterns in numbers on this chart (itself a good

1	2	3	4	5	6	7	8	9	10
11	12	13	14	15	16	17	18	19	20
21	22	23	24	25	26	27	28	29	30
31	32	33	34	35	36	37	38	39	40
41	42	43	44	45	46	47	48	49	50
51	52	53	54	55	56	57	58	59	60
61	62	63	64	65	66	67	68	69	70
71	72	73	74	75	76	77	78	79	80
81	82	83	84	85	86	87	88	89	90
91	92	93	94	95	96	97	98	99	100

Figure 2–9 *Computing with the Hundred Chart*

idea), she asked students what operation would be required to move between numbers. "What if I'm at 75 and I go to 65; what did I do?" The most obvious paths were to move directly up one row, which amounted to subtracting once by 10, or to move left by single units and subtract one from 75 ten times (see Figure 2–9).

Children began to look at more complex moves, such as the result of $25 \downarrow\downarrow\rightarrow$, where each arrow represented a directional move down rows and across columns; that is, $25 \downarrow\downarrow\rightarrow$ meant to move down 2 rows ($\downarrow\downarrow$) and right 1 column ($\rightarrow$). In that case, $25 \downarrow\downarrow\rightarrow$ meant $25 + 10 + 10 + 1$. As students continued these types of problems, they began to notice generalizations about their directional moves. For example, they quickly saw that $64 \rightarrow\downarrow$ (or $64 + 1 + 10$) was equivalent to $64 \downarrow\rightarrow$ (or $64 + 10 + 1$) and that the result of $46 \downarrow\downarrow\uparrow\uparrow$ was 46 because "when you add 20 and subtract 20, you're adding nothing."

Where is the algebraic thinking in this? In essence, children were doing computations without arithmetic by thinking structurally about operations on numbers. For example, with $46 \downarrow\downarrow\uparrow\uparrow$, they did not actually compute $46 + 10 + 10 - 10 - 10$. Instead, they analyzed the structure of the moves: From 46, two moves down followed by two moves up resulted in 46. Their reasoning that "when you add 20 and subtract 20, you're adding nothing" is a starting point for generalizing that "any number subtracted from itself is zero" or its symbolic form, $a - a = 0$,[7] where a represents a (real) number.

Conclusion

This chapter illustrates a variety of ways algebraic thinking can be integrated—in uncomplicated ways—into the arithmetic you are already teaching. These are just a few of many possibilities. As you become more skilled at identifying ways to find the algebra in arithmetic, your repertoire will grow. To help you get started, the ideas for making connections between arithmetic and algebra described in this chapter are summarized here:

- Look for important arithmetic properties to generalize.

- Design computation problems that aren't randomly generated, but that can lead to generalizations about properties of number and operation.

- Generalize about sums and products of evens and odds.

- Make known quantities unknown in arithmetic tasks by removing information.

- Vary known quantities in arithmetic tasks to create a set of number sentences that have a generalized solution.

- Help children build an algebraic view of equality.

- Ask students to express single-numerical-value solutions as unexecuted operations (e.g., as the sum of two numbers) so they learn that the answer is not always a single numerical value.

- Symbolize and solve missing number sentences.

- Look for ways to naturally introduce symbols into children's thinking. When tasks have unknown amounts (e.g., How Many Chickens?, Candy Problem), help children symbolize these unknowns.

---

[7]Don't underestimate what your children can do! For example, see Carpenter, Franke, and Levi (2003) for second grader Susie's reasoning that $a + b - b = a$ is a true conjecture.

CHAPTER 3

Functional Thinking in the Elementary Grades

As we saw in Chapter 2, you can build algebraic thinking into instruction by generalizing arithmetic. Another essential way to integrate early algebra is through *functional thinking*. Functional thinking is a process of building, describing, and reasoning with and about functions. It involves algebraic thinking because it includes *making a generalization* about how data are related.

Functional thinking is central to many areas of science that make our lives safer and simpler. For example, functions are used to understand and model many real-world phenomena, such as population growth, weather patterns, economic conditions, ground water contamination, or the structural stability in airplanes, buildings, and bridges. These functions, in turn, give us the ability to predict how the phenomena will behave under certain conditions. What path will a hurricane take? What will happen to a species if a deadly virus is introduced? How will contaminants dumped into a landfill affect water safety for surrounding residents? How will an earthquake affect the stability of a bridge? As our scientific understanding of the world becomes more complex, we need students who are better prepared to think about these complexities. This involves an understanding of functions and how they behave.

Understanding Functional Thinking

The *Principles and Standards for School Mathematics* (NCTM 2000) states that algebra in elementary grades should, over time, help children learn processes such as

- describing and extending generalizations about geometric and numeric patterns, including understanding how both repeating and growing patterns are generated;

- representing and analyzing patterns and functions using words, symbols, tables, and graphs and translating between these multiple representations;

- representing the idea of a variable as an unknown quantity using a letter or nonliteral symbol;

- investigating how a change in one variable relates to a change in the second variable; and

- looking for and applying relationships between varying quantities to make predictions.

This chapter examines what these components of functional thinking mean mathematically and what they look like in children's thinking.

As you encounter the functional thinking tasks in this chapter and throughout the remainder of the book, remember to take time to solve them before continuing your reading. This will help prepare your thinking for the discussions in the reading. As an additional help, you will find solutions to many of the tasks in the appendices. While only one solution is given for each task, you (and your students) might express your solutions in different ways.

Counting Dog Eyes

Functions are at the heart of functional thinking. A *function* is a mathematical statement that describes how two (or more) quantities vary in relation to each other. The relationship can range from very simple to very complex. It can be described in words or mathematical symbols, and it can be portrayed through representations like graphs and tables. Although there are many types of relationships between quantities, functions are special because they reflect a particular type of correspondence between two quantities. That is, in a function, each value of one quantity (let's call this the first quantity) corresponds or is related uniquely to a value of the second quantity.[1]

To understand what this means, let's begin with a simple illustration. Suppose you wanted to describe the total number of eyes that seven

---

[1] A formal treatment of functions can be found in many mathematics textbooks at or beyond secondary school grade level. This book looks specifically at relationships that are functions.

dogs have. Because you know the number of dogs, you can find the total number of eyes through a simple computation. You can either add 2 repeatedly (seven times) or multiply the number of dogs (seven) by 2. But this task has limited application because it only tells us the number of eyes for a specific number of dogs. What if you didn't know the number of dogs? Or knew that the number of dogs was a varying quantity that changed daily? (Perhaps the dogs are at an animal shelter where they are regularly adopted to families, so the amount of dogs at any particular time can vary.) How would you describe the total number of eyes in comparison to the number of dogs? You might express this relationship in words as "The total number of eyes is equal to the number of dogs multiplied by 2," or in symbols as $E = 2 \times n$, where n represents the number of dogs and E represents the number of eyes for n dogs.[2] Note that a particular number of dogs yields a unique value for the number of eyes. For example, 3 dogs correspond to exactly 6 eyes (assuming each dog has 2 eyes!). Thus, the correspondence between the number of dogs and eyes is the special relationship known as a function.

Regardless of how you represent this relationship, or function, its power is that it allows you to find the total number of eyes *for any number of dogs*. Let's use this simple function to more closely examine different aspects of functional thinking and the kinds of tools children can use to help them think about functions.

Looking Down or Looking Across?

To find the total number of eyes for any number of dogs, you might first describe how specific values of the two quantities—*the number of dogs* and *the number of eyes*—vary in relation to each other. For example, 1 dog has 2 eyes, 2 dogs have 4 eyes, 3 dogs have 6 eyes, and so on. We say these two quantities vary simultaneously because as the number of dogs increases, the number of eyes increases as well. Change in one quantity produces change in the other quantity. Finding the functional relationship between them involves identifying and describing what that change looks like *in general*. To do this, it is helpful to organize the data in a function table (see Figure 3–1).

Because the number of eyes depends on the number of dogs, we say that the number of eyes is the *dependent variable* and the number of dogs is the *independent variable*. While young children aren't necessarily

---

[2]After elementary grades, the expression $2 \times n$ is typically written as $2n$, without the symbol $\times$. Both notations are used here.

number of dogs	number of eyes
1	2
2	4
3	6

Figure 3-1 *Function table for dog eyes data*

expected to use this terminology (instead, the independent variable is sometimes informally referred to as "input" and the dependent variable as "output") it is important for them to be aware of how one quantity depends on another. Function tables help make this dependency explicit or visible because the independent variable (here, the number of dogs) is always recorded in the first column and the dependent variable in the second column (see Figure 3–2). This convention helps students visually organize the data into meaningful parts.

What children—and teachers—do with information in a function table varies. The first response is often to find a *recursive pattern*, which involves looking for a relationship within a sequence of values. If the task is to describe the number of dog eyes, recursive patterning would focus on the number of dog eyes (second column, or dependent variable) and leave the number of

independent variable	dependent variable
.	.
.	.
.	.
.	.
.	.
.	.

Figure 3-2 *Structure of a function table*

number of dogs	number of dog eyes
1	2 ⌐ +2
2	4 ←
3	6 ← +2
	?

Figure 3–3 *Focusing on a recursive pattern*

dogs (first column, or independent variable) implicit (see Figure 3–3). In other words, recursive patterning involves finding a pattern in the sequence of values 2, 4, 6 . . . by exploring questions such as, What operation can we perform on 2 to get 4, and then 4 to get 6? and Using this information, can we predict what value would come after 6? But the pattern leaves the number of dogs hidden because it does not connect this quantity to the number of dog eyes. Children often describe the recursive pattern in words as "add two every time." But they might not describe specifically how the number of dogs is connected to this pattern. In fact, in patterning problems in the early elementary grades, the independent variable is often not discussed or written about. This approach can limit the depth of functional thinking that students attain.

The significant feature of recursive patterning is that finding the pattern involves looking for a relationship in a sequence of values. In a function table, this means *looking down* the second column containing the number of dog eyes (the dependent variable). The number of dogs is not an explicit, visible part of this task. But what if you wanted to know the number of eyes for 200 dogs and you only had the recursive pattern "add two every time"? You would need to find the number of eyes for *all 200 dogs* by adding two to each consecutive total number of eyes. In other words, with recursive patterns, finding a particular value in a sequence requires knowing all of the values before it. Children quickly recognize that this is not the best approach for large numbers such as 200. It is too cumbersome. So, while recursive patterns are useful, they can limit the kinds of mathematical questions you might ask.

We can remedy this by getting children to *look across* the function table and think about how the two quantities correspond to each other. As illustrated in Figure 3–4, when the number of dogs increases by 1, the number of

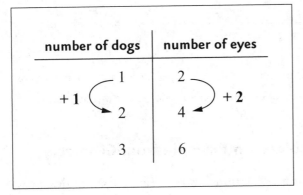

Figure 3-4 *Co-variation in a function table*

eyes increases by 2. This shift from *looking down* to *looking across* helps us understand how these quantities change in relation to each other, or *co-vary*.

We can take this horizontal analysis between the columns further by finding a *correspondence* between the quantities. This requires us to think about what operation on a particular number of dogs leads to the corresponding number of eyes. That is, what must be done to 1 (dog) to get 2 (eyes), or 2 (dogs) to get 4 (eyes)? For this simple multiplicative relationship, children as early as first grade can see that they must "double" the number of dogs, and in later grades, "multiply by two" (Blanton and Kaput 2005b). (See Figure 3–5.) They might express this relationship in natural language as "the number of dog eyes is double the number of dogs." By second and third grades, they can begin to express this correspondence symbolically. For example, if they represent the number of eyes as E and the number of dogs as n, then the function can be described as $E = 2 \times n$ (or $E = 2n$).[3]

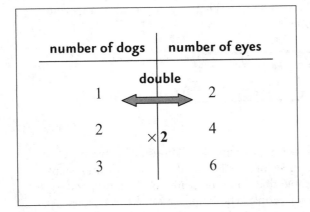

Figure 3-5 *Correspondence in a function table*

---

[3]The choice of E and n was arbitrary. Ask your students what symbols they want to use to represent these (and other) quantities.

TEACHER TASK 3.1

Find a function that describes the number of eyes and tails on *n* dogs. Express your function in words and symbols. How do you know it works?

The Trapezoid Table Problem: An Example from Geometry

Now that we've explored a simple relationship between dogs and dog eyes, let's consider the Trapezoid Table Problem (see Figure 3–6; also, see Appendix A, page 186, for a solution). It is included here because its mathematical structure is similar to the function in Counting Dog Eyes (both are *linear* functions, as we will see later), but also because it is an example of a task that brings geometry into the problem design.

Trapezoid Table Problem

Suppose you could seat 5 people at a table shaped like a trapezoid.

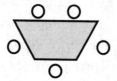

Figure 1

If you joined two trapezoid tables end to end (see Figure 2) how many people could you seat at the new table? What if you joined 3 trapezoid tables end to end? Four tables?

Figure 2

Organize your data in a table. Can you find a relationship between the number of tables and the number of people seated? Use this relationship to predict the number of people that could be seated at 20 tables and 100 tables. Describe the number of people who could be seated at *t* tables.

How do you know your relationship works?

Figure 3-6 *The Trapezoid Table Problem*

number of tables	number of people
1	5
2	8
3	11
4	14

Figure 3–7 *Function table for the Trapezoid Table
Problem*

A function table for this problem might look like the table in Figure 3–7. Looking down the second column at the number of people that can be seated, you probably notice a recursive pattern of "add 3." While this relationship is helpful, what we want is a function rule describing a relationship *between* the number of tables and the number of people. Reasoning from the table design and seating arrangement, we see that regardless of the number of tables, each table would seat 3 people on the sides, not counting the ends (see Figure 3–8). So, one table has 3 people seated on the sides, 2 tables have 6 people on the sides, 3 tables have 9 people on the sides, and *t* tables have 3 × *t* (or 3*t*) people seated on the sides. Also, there will always be 1 person seated on each end of the adjoined tables, contributing 2 additional people to the total number of persons seated (see Figure 3–9).

This reasoning leads to a function rule that might be described in natural language as "the number of people that can be seated is always 3

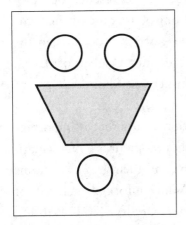

Figure 3–8 *Side seating on a
trapezoid table*

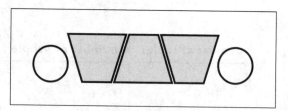

Figure 3–9 *End seating on a table of 3
adjoined trapezoids*

times the number of tables plus 2." You can write this symbolically as $P = 3t + 2$, where P is the total number of people and t is the number of tables. You can then use this rule to find that the number of people that can be seated at 20 tables is $3(20) + 2$, or 62, and the number of people that can be seated at 100 tables is $3(100) + 2$, or 302.

THINK ABOUT IT 3.1

How would the function change if you used a different geometric figure (e.g., square, triangle, pentagon) with the condition that only one person could be seated on each side or end? (See Appendix C, page 196, for an explanation.)

Functional Thinking Is a Critical Part of Mathematical Development

The power of a functional relationship (as opposed to a recursive pattern) is that it allows us to determine the value of a quantity at any point without knowing previous values. For example, if we are counting dog eyes, we can use the function rule $E = 2n$ (where E represents the number of eyes and n represents the number of dogs), to quickly find the number of eyes for any number of dogs: If there are 200 dogs, then the number of dog eyes is 2×200, or 400. We do not need information about values of the dependent variable (output) less than 200 as we would with recursive patterns.

But it's not just the ability to compute function values that is important in functional thinking. In later years, as students become more mathematically mature, they will learn to analyze functions and their graphs in terms of how quantities are changing or growing. While informal analyses of growth and change should begin in the elementary grades (NCTM 2000), many students encounter this type of analysis more formally in high school algebra courses and, later, calculus courses. It is this type of analysis that helps scientists understand how real-world phenomena behave and how to affect that behavior. Thus, functional thinking is a critical part of mathematical development, and introducing informal ideas about functions in elementary grades allows students the time and space to develop a more complex understanding than they might otherwise have if they first encounter functions in secondary grades.

Tools for Building, Analyzing, and Representing Functions

Children in elementary grades can develop tools to help them build, analyze, and represent functions. Tools are objects through which children create and express understanding. They come in many forms. With functions, they might be pictures, function tables, graphs, manipulatives, mathematical symbols, or even children's natural language. Children's understanding of functions will deepen as they develop the ability to use a variety of tools and understand the connections among them.

Function Tables

As we saw earlier, function tables can help children organize information about two varying quantities in a way that preserves important relationships in the data. Corresponding values of two quantities are listed in the same row (see Figure 3–10), and values of a particular quantity are listed in the same column (see Figure 3–11).

In the early elementary grades, even as early as kindergarten, function tables can serve both arithmetic and algebraic purposes. While you will

number of dogs	number of eyes
1	2
2	4
3	6

Figure 3-10 *Corresponding values in a function table (shaded)*

number of dogs	number of eyes
1	2
2	4
3	6

Figure 3–11 *Values for the number of dogs
(shaded)*

initially need to scaffold their thinking, children quickly learn to use function tables to organize data. Ideas about functions are in the background as young children learn to describe the number of objects in a collection, such as the number of eyes for two dogs, and record this in a table. Indeed, the challenge for kindergarten students is more likely to be counting eyes as they build arithmetic understanding about correspondence between sets and one-to-one relationships.

The goal is not just learning to count, but learning to count quantities that are related to each other (number of dogs and number of dog eyes) and preserving this relationship by way of a structure, such as a function table, that keeps this information visible. As children record numerals in a table, they also begin to work on ideas of correspondence between quantities because they are attending to *where* these numbers go in the table and the meanings embodied in the position of the numbers. They learn that certain numbers go in the first column and others in the second column. They learn that when they record a 2 for the number of dogs, they also record 4 for the number of dog eyes in the corresponding position in the next column. This process helps children begin to visually and cognitively look across columns and keep track of two quantities simultaneously, an important early step in functional thinking.

By first and second grade, the teacher's role in the use of function tables becomes less visible as children begin to recognize where and how to use this tool to organize data. Children become the recorders. Moreover, as they develop meaning for this tool, they are able to shift their focus to relationships in the data. Figure 3–12 depicts a first grader's function table for the Handshake Problem and her preliminary analysis of differences in the data.

By third grade, children can use function tables to actively reason about functional relationships.

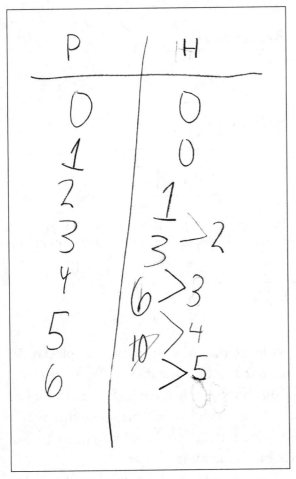

Figure 3–12 *A first grader's function table for
the Handshake Problem*

Third-grade teacher Angela Gardiner described how function tables helped her students build and analyze a functional relationship. She had designed a task (see Figure 3–13; also, see Appendix A, page 173, for a solution) that required finding the number of body parts a growing snake would have on Day 10 and on Day *n*. Each triangle (including the head) represented a body part. During class, she drew the growing snake on the board for Days 1, 2, and 3.

The class worked on this problem for approximately ten minutes. All organized their data with a T-chart.[4] When I pulled the group together to discuss the problem, it was Callie who had her hand waving hard. . . . Callie usually just sits and listens during math time, so her enthusiasm

---

[4]Function tables are sometimes called T-charts.

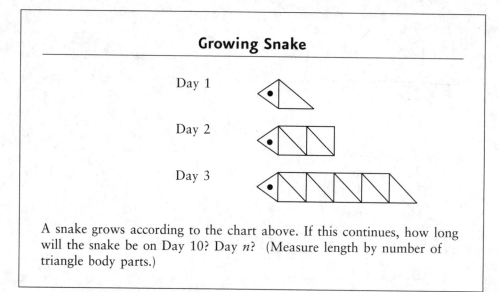

A snake grows according to the chart above. If this continues, how long will the snake be on Day 10? Day *n*? (Measure length by number of triangle body parts.)

Figure 3–13 *Growing Snake Problem*

was very special. I called on her right away. "I know that on day 10 the snake will have 101 body parts and I know that on day *n* the snake will have *n**n + 1.[5] I know this because I used my T-chart and I looked for the relationship between *n* and body parts. This is the first time I saw the pattern, so please tell me I'm right!" she said excitedly....The class had all come to pretty much the same answer.

Angela Gardiner, third-grade teacher

Callie explained that a function table helped her find and describe a relationship in the data ("I know this because I used my T-chart and I looked for the relationship between *n* and body parts"). She understood that the placement of numbers in the table preserved information about how the numbers were connected, and she used this to determine that the number of body parts on Day *n* would be $n \times n + 1$.

From Words to Symbols

As children become more sophisticated mathematical thinkers, they can move from the use of natural language descriptors ("the number of dogs") to more symbolic language (*D* for the number of dogs) to describe or represent quantities and relationships. When children explore quantities and

---

[5]Angela used the notation * to indicate multiplication.

how they relate, they start to appreciate that describing their ideas using natural language can be cumbersome, and that long phrases such as "the number of dogs," or even "dogs," might be simplified by the use of letters to symbolize a quantity (D for the number of dogs). Callie, for example, found it preferable to express the number of body parts on the growing snake as $n \times n + 1$, rather than as "the number of days times the number of days, plus 1." While it is true that Callie's teacher had suggested the use of n in the statement of the problem, her students had been working with symbols for some time. As a result, this had become a natural way for them to think about quantities such as the number of body parts for a snake.

Although there is not a magic age at which the transition from natural language to symbolic language occurs, classroom studies suggest that students can learn to use letters (or other nonliteral symbols) to represent unknown or varying quantities as they move into second and third grades. (Angela Gardiner's reflections in this chapter about the tasks Growing Snake and Growing Caterpillar illustrate this [see page 42].) Some research shows that it can happen in even earlier grades (see Dougherty 2008).

First-grade teacher Fran Vincent wrote about how her students used symbols to represent varying quantities in the Handshake Problem (see Figure 4–2, page 59):

> I asked, "Can I label one side [of the T-chart] *people* and the other side *handshake*?" One little boy said, "Just write p and h." I immediately stopped what I was doing. I asked, "What did you say?" He continued to repeat what I heard him say. "Awesome, how did you come up with that?" I probed. He continued, "Well, *people* begins with p and *handshakes* begin with h."

This is not to say that when children use letters to symbolize quantities or relationships they have a full understanding of what these letters, as *variables*,[6] represent. The notion of variable as either an unknown quantity (such as the value of x in the equation $9 + 3 = x + 4$) or as a quantity that can take on a range of values (such as the number of dogs) is not a simple concept. It takes time and experience to build a rich understanding of the notion of variable, particularly its meaning in a functional relationship (NCTM 2000). However, it is as students experience ways of talking and writing

---

[6]The term *variable* is used here inclusively to represent either an unknown or varying quantity. Some take the notion of variable to represent only a varying quantity.

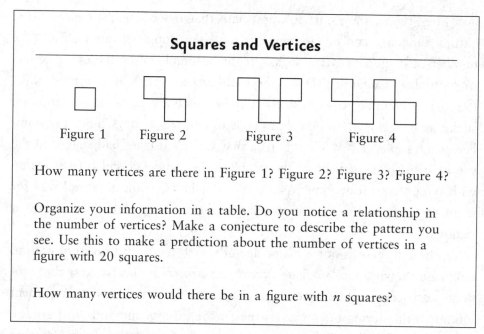

Squares and Vertices

Figure 1   Figure 2   Figure 3   Figure 4

How many vertices are there in Figure 1? Figure 2? Figure 3? Figure 4?

Organize your information in a table. Do you notice a relationship in the number of vertices? Make a conjecture to describe the pattern you see. Use this to make a prediction about the number of vertices in a figure with 20 squares.

How many vertices would there be in a figure with *n* squares?

Figure 3–14 *Squares and Vertices Problem* (Adapted from NCTM 1997, *Mathematics Teaching in the Middle School*, 4)

about relationships between quantities in symbolic ways that they begin to construct an understanding of variable. In this sense, teachers play a critical role because they can scaffold how children express their mathematical ideas so that their language becomes more sophisticated, more concise, more symbolic over time. Laura Panell wrote about guiding her fifth-grade students to transform their words into symbols on the task Squares and Vertices (Figure 3–14; see also Appendix A, page 181, for a solution):

> I directed my class to try and form a natural language statement about the function rule they had just discovered. Trenton raised his hand and stated, "You have to take the number of squares and multiply it by three and add one. This will give you the number of vertices." "OK," I said. "Let's see if we can revise this sentence to see if we can clean it up a bit." As a class, my students worked in groups to arrive at the conjecture "Multiply the number of squares by 3 and then add 1." I asked, "Do you think we can make a number sentence from this conjecture?" My students actively went to work. I gave them a few minutes and asked if anyone wanted to come up to the board and write their number sentence. Seth went up to the board and wrote, $S \times 3 + 1 = V$, where S represented the number of squares and V the number of vertices. "Great," I said. "Did anyone else have something different?" Trenton went up to the board and wrote, ☺ $\times 3 + 1 =$ ♥ where ☺ represented the number

of squares and ♥ the number of vertices. "All right," I said. "Even though Seth and Trenton had what appear to be different answers, are they both correct?" "Yes," Will said. "Trenton just used pictures instead of letters."

Laura asked her students to initially describe the functional relationship using natural language. She then guided their thinking toward more symbolic forms. It is important to keep in mind that children bring natural language skills to the mathematics classroom, and these skills are a tool by which they initially make sense of and talk about mathematics. Use these skills as a springboard for developing a more symbolic language so that it grows out of and is connected to a language that is more meaningful for children.

Visual Tools

For many children, a picture might indeed be worth a thousand words. Pictures, charts, graphs, and other types of visual representations are important tools for modeling, recording, synthesizing, or communicating mathematical information, including information about functions. In early elementary grades, children rely on pictures to help them reason about data, model situations, or keep important information visible (see Figure 3–15).

Figure 3–15 *A first grader draws faces to help her count and track the number of handshakes*

The drawings might be primitive, but they are an important part of children's reasoning. As a means of representation, they "make mathematical ideas more concrete and available for reflection" (NCTM 2000, 137).

In Counting Dog Eyes and the related task Counting Eyes and Tails (see Appendix A, page 162, for a solution of both tasks), kindergarten students drew and painted groups of dogs. Underneath their drawings, they recorded number sentences representing total eyes or total eyes and tails, then drew dots and marks representing eyes and tails (see Figure 3–16). For these young children, the visual representation of dogs, dots, and marks was an important way to keep information visible so that they could focus on mathematical ideas. Without the ability to make and use representations like this, the cognitive load of keeping everything in memory can hinder children's mathematical reasoning.

Under your guidance, as children mature mathematically, so can the visual tools they use. By third grade, children can graph functions that

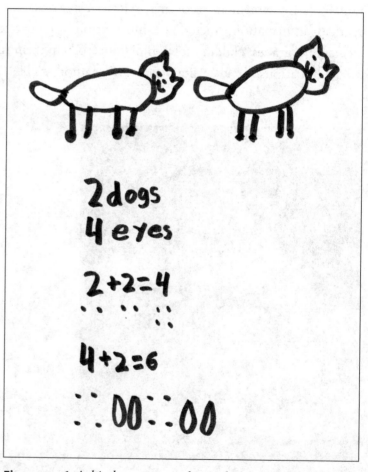

Figure 3–16 *A kindergarten student's drawing to depict the number of eyes or eyes and tails for two dogs*

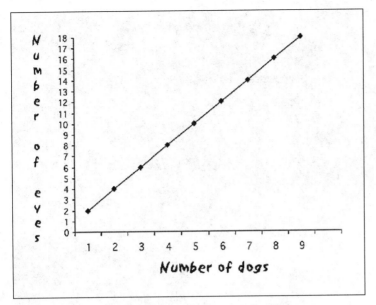

Figure 3–17 *Third graders' graph of the functional relationship between number of dogs and number of eyes*

coordinate the relationship between quantities. Figure 3–17 illustrates a
(Cartesian) graph constructed by third graders to show the relationship
between the numbers of dogs and eyes in Counting Dog Eyes. Figure 3–18
shows third graders discussing a frequency distribution graph representing
the relationship between the number of telephone calls made among a
group of friends and the number of friends in the group (see Figure 7–1,
page 124, for the Telephone Problem; see also Appendix A, page 183, for
a solution).

You don't need to limit graphing tools to conventional forms such as
these. Monk (2003) notes, "Another alternative to conventional graphing is
to encourage students to invent their own representations" (259). Figure
3–16 is an example of a student-invented representation of data for Counting Dog Eyes. While this representation does not coordinate data in the way
a Cartesian graph or frequency distribution might, it does suggest that the
power of alternative graphing forms (or, more generally, representations) is
that they hold significant meaning for the children who invent them.

Conventional and student-invented graphs are important tools for reasoning about functions because they offer children a different—visual—way
to access the information in a functional relationship. Some children will
prefer function tables, some will find symbolic representations of functions
more meaningful, but some will better understand a functional relationship
if it is communicated visually through a graph. Regardless of the particular form they prefer, keep in mind that children will have a richer, more

Figure 3–18 *Third graders use multiple representations in the Telephone Problem*

connected understanding of functions if they are able to navigate among *all* these forms of representation: words, symbols, tables, and graphs.

Finally, note that function graphs are important because, as students study more advanced mathematics in secondary grades and beyond, they learn to interpret critical information contained in the shape of the graph. Different types of functions have different graphical representations, and understanding these differences is an important part of understanding the mathematics of growth and change and, ultimately, more formal ideas of calculus. Elementary grades, then, become an important setting for children to begin to learn to construct and use visual tools such as graphs.

Children Thinking, Talking, and Writing About Functions

An important premise of early algebra is that elementary students can and should think about, describe, and reason with functions (NCTM 2000). Moreover, as this chapter points out, functional thinking is not just for the later elementary grades. Children in early elementary grades can begin to focus on relationships *between* quantities in addition to finding recursive patterns. They can learn how to represent and organize data in function tables. They can draw pictures to model and support their reasoning. They can learn to describe simple relationships between two quantities using everyday language. When teachers help children organize data in function tables and encourage them to look *across* the table for relationships, kindergarten and first-grade students can begin to describe functional relationships such as "every time we add one more dog we get two more eyes" or "it doubles." And, as we will see in this section, when children encounter ideas about functions in later elementary grades, they can learn to reason in even more mathematically sophisticated ways.

First Graders Reason About Cutting String

Julie Boardman adapted the task Cutting String[7] (see Figure 3–19; see also Appendix A, page 163, for a solution) for her first grade students to solve. After Julie had helped her class make 1 cut, then 2 cuts, and then discussed the results, she let them work individually to find the number of pieces of string after 3 cuts and use this to find a relationship between the number of cuts and the pieces of string. She wrote about their reasoning:

> I gave each student another piece of string. I also gave them each a piece of paper. I said, "Now we have seen how many pieces of string we'll get for one snip, and we have seen how many pieces of string we'll get for two snips. This information that we have found out is very important. What can we do to make sure that we don't forget what we know?" One child offered, "We can write it on the paper." I said, "Yeah, sure! And why would we want to do this?" Rachael said, "So we know how many snips and how many strings we got from it."
>
> I told them that they would now be thinking about how many pieces of string they would get from three snips. I told them to make sure they recorded what they found out on their paper. I encouraged them to show me their findings in whatever way they wanted: in pictures, numbers or words. Natalie said, "We can make a T-chart."

---

[7]Keep in mind that functional thinking tasks that have a physical context (such as cutting string or folding paper) might have physical limitations that the functional relationship does not necessarily account for. For example, the functional relationship for Cutting String can be evaluated for any number of cuts on a piece of string. But what are the physical constraints for, say, one million cuts of a piece of string? If the task involves folding a piece of paper (see Figure 4–15, page 76), how many folds are physically possible before the size and width of the paper become an issue? Depending on your students, you might want to explore the contrasts between finding a functional relationship that theoretically holds for any value of the independent variable (for example, for any number of cuts or any number of folds) and the limitations imposed by the physical context of the problem you are modeling.

Cutting String

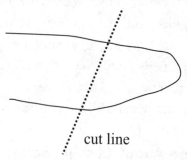

cut line

Fold a piece of string to make one loop. While it is folded, make 1 cut (see figure). How many pieces of string do you have? Fold another piece of string to make one loop. Make 2 cuts and find the number of pieces of string. Repeat for 3, 4, and 5 cuts.

How many pieces of string do you get for each number of cuts? Organize your data in a table.

What patterns do you notice in your data?

What can you say about the relationship between the number of cuts and the number of pieces of string? Write your conjecture in words or symbols.

Without cutting the string, use this relationship to predict the number of pieces that would result from 6 cuts. What about 100 cuts?

Figure 3–19 *Cutting String Problem*

Many of the students were able to find out how many pieces of string they would get after three snips. Once they had their recordings, I demonstrated cutting the string three times and as a group we found out how many pieces of string resulted. After this part of the task, I asked my students what they noticed about the amount of strings they were getting each time. Jamie replied, "It gets 2 more each time." I said, "That's right. And how many snips are we making each time?" He said, "One more each time."

I then told the class to make a prediction about how many strings they would get if they made four snips. I told them that they would not be getting a string this time. They would have to use what they knew about the other pieces of string to figure out how many pieces they would get for four snips. There were a few children who shouted the answer out right away. "Nine!" I was pleased that they knew, but I still wanted them to justify their answer. When I asked Jamie how he knew there would be nine pieces of string, he replied, "Because you get two more each time." I said, "Two more of what?" He replied, "Strings." I asked him how we could prove that. He said that we could cut the string to find out. I gave him another string and he cut it four times. He then proceeded to count them and got nine. Jamie was thinking algebraically. He found the pattern and, without realizing it, was able to conjecture that there would be two more pieces of string for every additional cut that was made.

I asked the students if we could make a conjecture about the pattern to help us find out how many pieces of string we would get for any number of snips. I reminded them that a conjecture is something we can say about the pattern we found. I also told them that we needed to see if our conjecture would work every time. I asked them, "What can you say about the pattern?" Tyra said, "It's strings." I said, "Yes. That's what we get. What do you notice about these numbers?" Jimma said, "It's two more each time." Rachael said, "It's like skip-counting." I said, "By what?" Rachael said, "Skip-counting by twos." I said, "Yeah, so if we know we're skip-counting by twos, and we wanted to find out how many pieces of string we would get for five snips, what can we say that would make it easier to find it out without actually making the snips with the string?" Jamie replied, "Every time you make one more snip it's two more." I said, "Two more than what?" He said, "Two more than the one before." I said, "Aha! So we would have to look back at the pattern." I wrote the conjecture that Jamie said: Every time you make one more snip you get two more pieces of string than you had before.

The reasoning that Julie's first graders applied to this task was impressive. They drew pictures to model the task, they understood that function tables were an important way to organize their data ("We can make a T-chart.") and were able to use these for this purpose, they were able to describe a recursive pattern using everyday language ("It's two more each time," "It's like skip-counting [by twos]"), they were able to make predictions based on this pattern, and they were able to extend their recursive pattern to a generalization that described a co-varying relationship in the data ("Every time you make one more snip you get two more pieces of string than you had before").

Julie's case demonstrates that by finding novel and creative ways to scaffold children's thinking about functions, teachers in grades K through two can build a critical foundation that will help children become more sophisticated mathematical thinkers in later elementary grades and beyond.

THINK ABOUT IT 3.2

Opportunities for algebraic thinking sometimes come up in unexpected places. The number of pieces of string generated from 1 cut, 2 cuts, 3 cuts, and so on, yields the sequence of values 3, 5, 7.... Children who know about odd numbers will likely recognize these values as odd. How can you use this as an opportunity to explore generalizations about odd (and even) numbers? You don't need to have a specific task designed. While children are solving Cutting String, you can ask questions informally to get them to generalize arithmetic.

THINK ABOUT IT 3.3

Do you think it is valuable for first graders to be able to reason about functions in the way described here? If you taught first grade, would you want your students to be able to reason like Julie's students? Why?

Functional Thinking in Later Elementary Grades

By third grade, children can think in even more advanced ways about functions and—like Julie's first graders—are deeply engaged by these ideas. In fact, children often describe early algebra tasks like Cutting String as "fun math" and are excited to solve these types of problems, even though the tasks are often more complex. As one fourth-grade student said, "I used to hate math, but now I love it!"

Let's look at how Angela Gardiner's third graders reasoned about Growing Caterpillar, a task Angela developed as a sequel to Growing Snake (see Figure 3–20; see also Appendix A, page 169, for a solution).

Angela wrote:

I showed my students my caterpillar example and all I wanted them to see was how I developed the problem. I had no idea that they would begin to solve the problem. I couldn't stop them. There were hands going up all over the place. Everyone wanted to tell me the pattern they saw

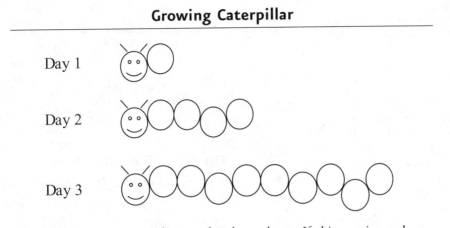

A caterpillar grows according to the chart above. If this continues, how long will the caterpillar be on Day 4? Day 5? Day 100? Day x? (Measure length by number of circle body parts.)

Figure 3–20 *Growing Caterpillar Problem*

when they looked at the growth of the caterpillar. I said, "Guys, I haven't even asked you the question yet." "But I see the pattern, Mrs. Gardiner," yelled Jak. "Okay, what do you think the pattern is?" I asked. "I think it is x times 2 plus one," he said. "How many of you agree with Jak?" I questioned. "I don't know. I have to do a T-chart," explained Meg. "Well, then let's do that together on the board," I said. With the students' help, we drew the following T-chart on the board (see Figure 3–21).

"Now that we have that on the board, I don't agree with Jak," said Meg. "Why is that, Meg?" I asked. "Because if it was x times 2 plus 1, then x would be 1 and y would be 3. And, it's not. It's $x = 1$ and $y = 2$," she explained. (If x equaled 1, then by Jak's formula, y would be $2(1) + 1$, or 3, not 2, as the T-chart indicated.) The class struggled with the pattern for a long time. Then Shane saw a pattern that I had not seen. He came up to the T-chart on the board and highlighted the pattern (see Figure 3–22). What Shane said was that if you add $1 + 2 + 2$, it equals 5. If you then add $2 + 5 + 3$, it equals 10. This didn't help him find the formula, but it did help Joe! "I see it, I know the formula!" Joe cried out. "Well, what is it?" I prodded. "It's $x*x + 1 = y$," he said. At that moment, a loud group of "Oh yeahs" could be heard in the room. I asked everyone why this was algebra. I think Jak put it best. He said, "Because we have people looking for patterns and relationships and we have them developing a formula."

x	y
1	2
2	5
3	10
4	17

Figure 3–21 *Function table for Growing Caterpillar, where x represents the number of days and y represents the number of body parts*

Angela's reflections on Growing Snake and Growing Caterpillar illustrate that third graders can think in sophisticated ways about how quantities relate, how to symbolize these relationships, and whether these conjectured relationships are valid. For instance, without guidance from Angela, Jak spontaneously proposed a symbolic relationship between an arbitrary day, *x*, and the number of caterpillar body parts, *y*. Meg was able to use the function table to refute Jak's conjecture ("Now that we have that on the board, I don't agree with Jak . . . because if it was *x* times 2 plus 1, then *x* would be one and *y* would be three. And, it's not. It's $x = 1$ and $y = 2$"). Joe then built on Shane's observation to conjecture another symbolic relationship ("It's $x*x + 1 = y$"), which the class accepted.

Angela's students had had little, if any, previous experience with functional thinking. Their success with these tasks suggests that the study of

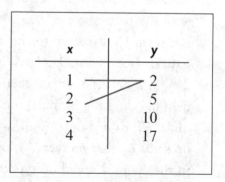

Figure 3–22 *Shane's observation about Growing Caterpillar*

simple functions (such as the relationship between the number of dogs and the number of dog eyes) in the earlier elementary grades could help build critical tools and thinking skills that would support the study of more complicated functions, such as those in Growing Snake and Growing Caterpillar, in later elementary grades.

Conclusion

This chapter focused on functional thinking as an important part of what it means to think algebraically. Functions help us make sense of the world in which we live and are a critical part of children's mathematical development. With the right kinds of tasks and instruction, children can learn to think in very sophisticated ways about how quantities relate to each other. As the next chapter more fully explores, it is easy to bring functional thinking into your classroom by building on the curriculum you already have in place. The result will help make children's mathematical experiences rewarding and fun.

CHAPTER 4

Building Functional Thinking into the Curriculum

Functional Thinking or Arithmetic?

So far, we have seen that functional thinking is an important and central topic in mathematics and that elementary school children are able to think in sophisticated ways about relationships between quantities.

But how can functional thinking become a regular part of classroom instruction in elementary schools? Although in more recent years new ideas set forth by the *Principles and Standards for School Mathematics* (NCTM 2000) do promote algebraic thinking, including work with functions, functional thinking has not historically been a central part of the curriculum in the elementary grades. And, while arithmetic *understanding* has received increased attention, instruction in some elementary schools still emphasizes learning number facts and arithmetic skills and procedures.

Although new standards-based curricula and resources are being developed to change the role of functional thinking in the elementary grades, for some teachers access to those changes may be too far down the road. As it is, teachers sometimes have limited resources, and schools might have a scripted curriculum in place. Moreover, even if teachers are free to draw from different resources and materials to supplement their school's agenda, they often feel the constraint of "covering the curriculum." Which topics are most important? Which ones can be eliminated?

Although these are real challenges that teachers face daily, it is critical to understand that, like generalized arithmetic, *functional thinking is not an additional set of topics to teach*. It is not a set of skills to be taught after children have mastered arithmetic. It does not require you to choose between helping students learn basic skills or think about more challenging math problems. As with all of algebraic thinking, functional thinking is about making elementary grades mathematics—including arithmetic—deeper and more meaningful for children. Tasks like Growing Snake or Counting Dog Eyes give children an exciting context for thinking about and practicing arithmetic. In turn, as Chapter 5 explains, arithmetic does not have to be a rote set of procedures, but can serve as a tool to help children analyze and describe functional relationships.

Developing Functional Thinking Tasks

Think of an Arithmetic Question

Building functional thinking tasks is simple, and you can start with the resources you have at hand. Think of an arithmetic question that involves counting a quantity that can change over time or vary in a natural way. The question might be about the number of dog eyes on 4 dogs, the number of different handshakes possible among 3 children, the number of outfits that can be made out of 2 shirts and 1 pair of pants,[1] the number of legs on a cow, or the number of grains of rice after 4 days if you start with one grain on the first day and double the amount you have on each successive day. The point is that these questions can be answered using arithmetic and perhaps some modeling process (such as drawing the possible outfits; see Figure 4–1).

Vary a Parameter

Once you've decided on an arithmetic question, think about how you might vary a parameter, or quantity, in the task. (The quantity you vary will represent the independent variable in the function.) You might vary the number of dogs, or the number of shirts, or the number of children shaking hands, or the number of cows, or the number of days you are collecting rice. For example, instead of just 2 shirts, what if you had 3 shirts? Or 4 shirts? Or 5 shirts? Or 200 shirts? How many outfits would you get each time? A change in each of these quantities (the independent variable) will result in a change in the quantity being counted (the dependent variable). Changing the number of children in a group will change the total number of handshakes. Changing the number of shirts will change the number of

---

[1]Assume that an outfit consists of 1 shirt and 1 pair of pants.

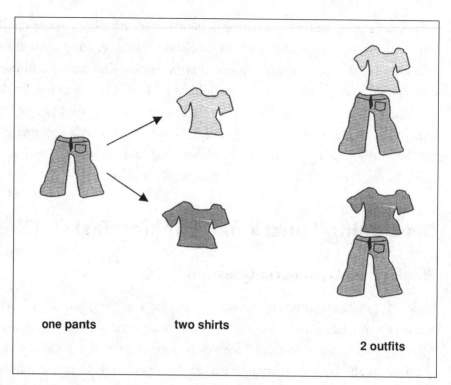

one pants   two shirts

2 outfits

Figure 4–1 *Possible outfits from 2 shirts and 1 pair of pants*

possible outfits. The goal is to think about and describe in words or symbols *how change in one quantity affects change in the second quantity.* The result represents the relationship between the two quantities.

Varying one parameter allows you to build a task that looks for a functional relationship between two quantities. The Handshake Problem illustrates the transition from an arithmetic task to one that requires algebraic (functional) thinking (see Figure 4–2).

THINK ABOUT IT 4.1

How many handshakes will there be if you have *n* people in your group? Express your function in words and symbols. How do you know it works? (See Appendix A, page 175, for a solution.)

I presented the Handshake Problem to my students. I was feeling nervous about this, but I knew my students were going to love it. I think it was during this problem that I realized students sometimes teach better than I do. It was during this problem that my classroom switched from teacher driven to student driven.

Angela Gardiner, third-grade teacher

Handshake Problem

Arithmetic Task:
How many handshakes will there be if 3 people shake hands, where each person shakes the hand of every person once? How did you get your answer? Show your solution on paper.

Extension:
How many handshakes will there be if 4 people shake hands?
How many handshakes will there be if 5 people shake hands?
How many handshakes will there be if 6 people shake hands?

Organize your data in a table. Do you see a relationship in the numbers?

How many handshakes will there be if 50 people shake hands? How did you get your answer? What can you say about the relationship between the number of people in a group and the total number of handshakes? Describe the relationship in words or symbols.

Figure 4-2 *Changing the Handshake Problem from an arithmetic task to one that uses algebraic thinking*

Use Numbers Algebraically

The numbers you choose for the values of the parameter you vary will depend on the age and experience of your students and the complexity of the pattern. Kindergarten children are just beginning to construct an understanding of number, so quantities such as 1, 2, and 3 are good starting points for them, while 10 might be an upper limit for the value of the parameter. For older children, upper limits can be much larger values.

Ultimately, the choice of number is not just about arithmetic. It is also a powerful way to help children think algebraically. For example, in the Handshake Problem, you might ask children to find the number of handshakes in a group of 3 children, 4 children, and 5 children. For each of these cases, the numbers are small enough that students can find the number of handshakes arithmetically by counting. But the goal is to move children beyond the arithmetic so that they begin to think algebraically about the structure and relationships in the numbers. Knowing the number of handshakes for a few cases only gives us information about those cases and does not allow us to think in broader terms about how the relationship, or function, behaves for any number of children in a group. Using numbers algebraically involves choosing a number for the highest value of your parameter that is small enough so that children will understand it but large enough that they will not be able to (or will not want to) solve the problem using arithmetic. In this way, large numbers can prompt children to think about structure and relationships in the numbers.

For example, if there are 100 children in a group, students do not have enough time (or patience!) to compute the total number of handshakes for 100 children by counting all the possibilities. Instead, teachers can help children answer questions such as "How many handshakes would there be if 100 children shook hands with each other once?" by looking at small, manageable cases (such as 3 children, 4 children, and so on), then using these cases to find a relationship between the number of children in the group and the total number of handshakes. That relationship provides a way to answer the question for 100 children.

TEACHER TASK 4.1

Consider the following arithmetic question. How many rectangles are in the given figure? (See Appendix B, page 190, for a solution.)

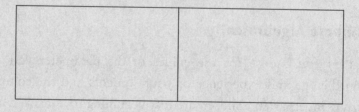

How can you transform this arithmetic task into one that involves functional thinking? (See Appendix A, page 167, for a solution.)

Look for a Generalization (Function Rule)

Once children generate the data and organize these values in a function table, such as in Figure 4–3, they can think about how the quantities relate to each other and look for a generalization (here, a function or function rule) to describe this relationship. Generalizations come from answers to questions such as, How many total handshakes would there be for a group of children *of any number*? How many outfits are possible given *any number of shirts* (and a fixed number of pairs of pants)? How many eyes would there be for a group of dogs *of any number*? How many vertices would there be for *any number of squares*?

number of children	number of handshakes
1	0
2	1
3	3
4	6
5	10
6	15

Figure 4-3 *A function table for the Handshake Problem*

A task like Counting Dog Eyes has a simple relationship that most children can describe in some form, such as "it doubles," "every time you add one more dog you get two more eyes," or "$E = 2D$," where E represents the number of eyes and D represents the number of dogs. However, the ease in finding these relationships will vary depending on children's experience and the difficulty of the problem. The process they use can vary as well. For example, children might develop a function based on their analysis of patterns in the data or try to reason from the context of the problem and use features of the task to develop a function (see "The Trapezoid Table Problem: An Example from Geometry," pages 36–38 for an example of reasoning from the problem's context).

Use Unexecuted Expressions to Help Find Functional Relationships

For more complicated relationships, we sometimes need creative ways to think about how they work. One type of problem where this is true is the Handshake Problem (Figure 4–2). Let's think about an alternative way for children to solve this task.

The practice in elementary grades is often to express answers as computed quantities, in the form of a specific number, rather than leaving them in their unexecuted form as a number sentence. Children interpret "answer" to mean a single numerical value. However, information that is useful for finding generalizations is sometimes lost through computation. For example, the handshake data (see Figure 4–3) tell us that there would be 6 handshakes for a group of 4 children. But how do we arrive at 6 handshakes? When children are systematic in how they shake hands, they can see that 6 comes from computing $3 + 2 + 1$ (or $1 + 2 + 3$), and $3 + 2 + 1$ reflects a pattern in how they physically acted out shaking hands (see Figure 4–4). That is, in a group of 4 children, Child A would shake hands with Children B, C, and D (3 handshakes), Child B would shake

Figure 4–4 *First graders act out shaking hands and record their results*

hands with Children C and D (2 handshakes), then Child C would shake hands with Child D (1 handshake).

THINK ABOUT IT 4.2

If you asked your students what "answer" meant, what would they say?

If children leave the number of handshakes in unexecuted form, they can analyze the relationship between the number of children in a group and the number of handshakes by looking at *the structure of each number sentence in comparison to the number of children for that particular sentence* (see Figure 4–5).

Third graders, for example, will notice that the number sentence describing the number of handshakes for 4 people begins with 3 (see Figure 4–5), for 5 people it begins with 4, and so on. In looking across the columns, they can attend to how the number of handshakes, as expressed by the number sentence, is related to the number of children. They might express the generalized relationship in words as "the total number of handshakes is the sum of the numbers from 1 up to one less than the number of children in the group." (For example, in a group of 10 children, the number of handshakes would be $1 + 2 + 3 + \cdots + 9$.) Or, children in

number of children	number of handshakes
1	0
2	1
3	3 $\quad= 2 + 1$
4	6 $\quad= 3 + 2 + 1$
5	10 $\quad= 4 + 3 + 2 + 1$
6	15 $\quad= 5 + 4 + 3 + 2 + 1$

Figure 4–5 *Handshake data in unexecuted form*

later elementary grades might express this symbolically: For a group of *n* children, the total number of handshakes is $1 + 2 + 3 + \cdots + (n - 1)$.

Finding a function rule to describe the handshake data can be more challenging. If the number of children in the group is *n*, then the total number of handshakes can be expressed in symbols as $\frac{n \times (n - 1)}{2}$. But, because computing the sum $1 + 2 + 3 + \cdots + (n - 1)$ would be difficult for large values of *n*, the expression $\frac{n \times (n - 1)}{2}$ is arguably a more powerful description. However, for some children, identifying this expression is complicated. The analysis of unexecuted sums, then, provides a useful intermediate step for generalizing a correspondence relationship in the data.

The Triangle Dot Problem is another task in which leaving number sentences in their unexecuted form can help children find a functional relationship (see Figure 4–6; see also Appendix A, page 185, for a solution). Although the task begins with a 5-dot triangle, it might be helpful for children to look first at cases for 3-dot and 4-dot triangles. This will allow them to build a set of data that can be organized in some way, such as through a table, in order to find a relationship to predict the total number of dots for a 13-dot triangle.

Rather than randomly counting dots, guide children to count the dots along one side of the triangle, record the amount, then count the dots on

---

Triangle Dot Problem

The figure below contains a drawing of a 5-dot triangle made by using 5 dots on each side. The 5-dot triangle requires a total of 12 dots to construct. How many dots will be used to make a 13-dot triangle?

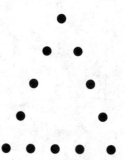

If *n* represents the number of dots on each side of an *n*-dot triangle, write an expression to represent the total number of dots in the triangle.

Figure 4–6 *Triangle Dot Problem* (NCTM 1997, *Mathematics Teaching in the Middle School, 2*)

the adjoining side and record this amount. Repeat this for the third side. Using these values, ask them to construct a number sentence that can be used to find the total number of dots but *do not compute this number sentence.* They will find that the total number of dots for the 3-dot triangle can be expressed as $3 + 2 + 1$, where the number sentence itself models and preserves the action of the counting. For the 4-dot triangle, the total number of dots is $4 + 3 + 2$.

If we examine the structure in these number sentences and compare it to the triangle dot number, we find an interesting relationship. For example, the total number of dots in a 3-dot triangle can be expressed as 3 plus the two (whole) numbers preceding 3: $3 + 2 + 1$. For the 4-dot, the total number of dots is 4 plus the two numbers preceding 4: $4 + 3 + 2$. In general, we can express the number of dots for an arbitrary triangle as the sum of three quantities: the triangle dot number plus the triangle dot number $- 1$ plus the triangle dot number $- 2$. If we let n denote the triangle dot number and d the total number of dots, we can express the relationship between the triangle dot number and the total number of dots symbolically as $d = n + (n - 1) + (n - 2)$. (Students in upper elementary grades might simplify this to $d = 3n - 3$.) The point is that the unexecuted sums preserve important information about the relationship between the triangle dot number and the total number of dots. If we computed the sums, that information would be hidden.

Keep in mind it is important *not* to solve this task using arithmetic. That is, children should avoid constructing a 13-dot triangle and counting the total number of dots. If your students try to solve this arithmetically, you can increase the number of dots to push them to think algebraically. Answering questions such as "How many dots are there in a 1,000-dot triangle?" would involve the use of triangles for which it is too cumbersome to draw and count dots. Of course, asking your students for the number of dots in an n-dot triangle will also get them to think algebraically.

? THINK ABOUT IT 4.3

It is important to remember that there are different ways to reason about and express solutions to a particular functional thinking task. Reasoning from the context (here, the physical model provided in Figure 4–6), can you think of another way to identify the functional relationship in the Triangle Dot Problem? (See Appendix C, page 198, for an explanation.)

Although leaving sums in their unexecuted form can be a useful tool for finding functional relationships, your students might be better able to identify the function by looking for patterns in data expressed in executed forms. The point is that offering students choices in how they can reason about data—whether through unexecuted sums or through data expressed in executed form—will increase their chances for success in functional thinking.

Finally, guide students to explore questions such as "Does it always work?" or "Why does it work?" Angela Gardiner's description of her class' solving the Growing Caterpillar Problem (pages 52–55) illustrates students' thinking about the accuracy of Jak's conjecture ("I think it is x times 2 plus 1") and, based on the evidence, deciding that his conjecture did not hold. Children should be given opportunities to examine their conjectures about functional relationships in order to convince themselves whether the conjectures hold true (see also Chapter 6).

Symbolize the Relationship

The goal in symbolizing relationships is to scaffold students' mathematical language so that it builds from their everyday language to more symbolic ways of speaking and writing. There are a few points to keep in mind. First, don't expect children to use symbols prematurely, that is, before they have any meaning associated with the symbols or the relationships to be symbolized. Instructing children to talk about n outfits or E dog eyes without giving them experiences in making sense of these symbols falls short of the goals of functional thinking. Children need opportunities to explore the relationships to be symbolized through their everyday language.

On the other hand, don't expect children to fully understand the meaning of a symbol before they use it. It is as children work with symbols that they acquire meaning for them. They will experience a natural progression in their thinking that begins with a limited understanding of symbols or symbolizing. The teacher's challenge is to balance this tension by scaffolding students' symbol sense over time, questioning children so that symbols emerge in the context of activity and as children see value in describing their ideas in more concise forms.

Design Tasks That Incorporate Important Mathematical Concepts

Tasks described here, such as Growing Snake or Growing Caterpillar (see Chapter 3), illustrate how to change arithmetic problems (count the number of body parts on a snake or caterpillar) into those that require functional

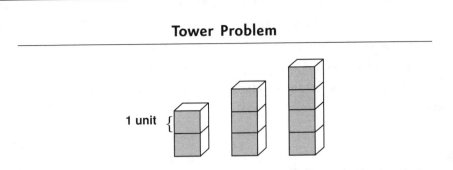

Tower Problem

1 unit {

What is the surface area of each tower of cubes (include the bottom)? As the tower gets taller, how does the surface area change? What is the surface area of a tower with 50 cubes?

Figure 4–7 *Tower Problem* (NCTM 2000, 160)

thinking (find a way to describe the number of body parts on a growing snake or growing caterpillar after *n* days). Tasks can also be designed to intentionally incorporate aspects of your curriculum other than arithmetic, such as geometry, probability, or measurement. The Tower Problem (Figure 4–7; see also Appendix A, page 184, for a solution) and the Spinner Problem (Figure 4–8; see also Appendix A, page 180, for a solution) illustrate this.

THINK ABOUT IT 4.4

What might the Tower Problem look like if it did not involve functional thinking? (See Appendix C, page 198, for a solution.)

Spinner Problem

If you create a spinner by dividing a circle in half, what is the probability that the arrow will land on any one section of the circle? What if you divide the circle into thirds? Fourths? Fifths? If you divide the circle into *n* pie-shaped regions of equal size, what is the probability that the arrow will land on any one of the sections? (Assume outcomes are equally likely.)

Figure 4–8 *Spinner Problem*

The Tower Problem uses the geometry of stacks of cubes to get students to think about surface area. Here, functional thinking supports the development of geometric concepts by giving students a context for thinking about surface area. Conversely, a task like the Tower Problem allows you to embed an important geometric concept—surface area—in algebraic thinking.

THINK ABOUT IT 4.5

What might the Spinner Problem look like if it did not involve functional thinking? (See Appendix C, page 198, for a solution.)

The Spinner Problem allows children to explore general principles for computing probabilities. While it is important for children to be able to compute a particular probability (such as the probability a spinner will land on one region of a circle divided in half), it is mathematically more powerful to explore what would happen over a variety of cases and use this to develop a general principle for computing probabilities.

These tasks are included here to demonstrate the flexibility that functional thinking can have. They are not limited to arithmetic, but can occur in geometry, probability, or any other context where relationships between quantities might be of interest.

Vary the Problem Design to Create a Family of Functional Thinking Tasks

Sometimes, the design of a task can be changed to generate a group of related tasks. Cutting String (page 49) is one such task. In that task, a piece of string was folded to create one loop (see Figure 4–9a). The goal was to find a relationship between the number of cuts across the loop (see Figure 4–9b) and the number of string pieces that resulted.

An interesting question to explore is how the relationship would change if there were *two* loops instead of one (see Figure 4–10; see also Appendix A, page 163, for a solution). If you vary the number of cuts as before (that is, 1 cut, 2 cuts, 3 cuts, . . . 100 cuts), what would the relationship between the number of cuts and the number of pieces of string be? This by itself is a stand-alone functional thinking task (see Figure 4–11) that does not require solving Cutting String.

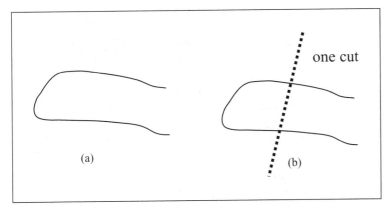

one cut

(a)   (b)

Figure 4–9 *A piece of string folded to make one loop*

TEACHER TASK 4.2

Solve the tasks Cutting String and Cutting a Two-Loop String. Express the functional relationships in words and symbols. Do you see any similarities between these two functions?

Of course, if we can vary the string configuration to make 2 loops, we can also vary it to make 3 loops (see Figure 4–12). What would happen to the functional relationship if there were 3 loops? Four loops? One hundred loops? (Or even n loops?)

TEACHER TASK 4.3

Based on the task Cutting a Two-Loop String, design tasks for Cutting a Three-Loop String and Cutting a Four-Loop String. Make sure you adapt the numbers (and wording) for your grade level. Solve each of these tasks.

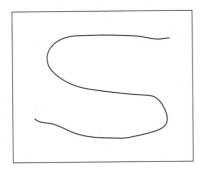

Figure 4–10 *A piece of string
folded to make two loops*

Cutting a Two-Loop String

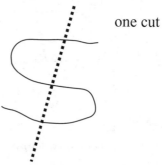

one cut

Fold a piece of string to make two loops. While it is folded, make 1 cut (see figure). How many pieces of string do you have? Fold another piece of string to make two loops. Make 2 cuts and find the number of pieces of string that results. Repeat this for 3, 4, and 5 cuts.

How many pieces of string do you have for each number of cuts? Organize your data in a table.

What patterns do you notice in your data?

What can you say about the relationship between the number of cuts and the number of pieces of string? Write your conjecture in words or symbols.

Without cutting the string, use this relationship to predict the number of pieces that would result from 6 cuts. Predict the number of pieces that would result from 100 cuts.

Figure 4–11 *Cutting a two-loop string*

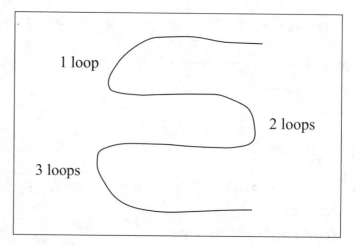

1 loop

2 loops

3 loops

Figure 4–12 *A string with three loops*

By changing the number of loops in the string, we generate a functional thinking task that can be solved independently of the others. The solution to each task—that is, the function describing the relationship between the number of cuts and the number of pieces of string—becomes part of a *family of functions* because of the similarity of their forms.

THINK ABOUT IT 4.6

You should now have four different functions representing solutions to the tasks created by looking at cuts for 1 loop, 2 loops, 3 loops, and 4 loops. Do you notice any similarities or differences in the four functions? What changes? What stays the same? Can you describe a pattern in the form of the functions? What can you say about the functional relationship for a string that has *n* loops? (See Appendix C, page 199, for an explanation.)

As you increase the number of loops, the complexity of the task increases. One approach is to give each of the tasks to your students over appropriate intervals of time, based on your discretion and knowledge of students. As children have time to explore the ideas in each of the tasks independently, they will be more prepared to look at commonalities across tasks. Even so, finding a relationship in the family of functions generated through these tasks could be challenging for your students. You will need to judge what is appropriate based on your own experience. You might want to reserve the analysis of commonalities across all the function solutions (Think About It 4.6, this page) as a challenge for children in upper elementary grades. Either way, these tasks are an excellent opportunity for you to build your own understanding of functions!

TEACHER TASK 4.4

Look through the curriculum you are teaching to find an idea that can be used to develop a functional thinking task. Use the principles described here to guide your thinking. Adapt the task to the grade level you teach. Solve the task, then let your students try it.

Scaffolding Functional Thinking Tasks

Finally, let's consider how you might scaffold functional thinking tasks in your classroom. The intent here is not to prescribe certain tasks for a particular grade. As Chapter 3 described, at different grades children will focus on various mathematical aspects of a task and, thus, can benefit from many or all of them. But there are some general guidelines that might help you get started.

Start with Tasks That Have Simple Functional Relationships

Start with simple relationships. The goal is for the relationship to be simple enough so that children can begin to focus on "looking across" in order to think about how two quantities vary in relation to each other or, at a minimum, recognize a recursive pattern. Counting Dog Eyes, which is based on the notion of doubling, is a task you might want to start with in the early elementary grades.

As another example, consider the task Saving for a Bicycle (see Figure 4–13; see also Appendix A, page 179, for a solution). Figure 4–14 shows a function table for this task where the output values (values of the dependent variable) have been given in their unexecuted form and also as computed sums. This representation can help children see that Saving for a Bicycle involves a simple relationship based on repeated addition of 3. With this representation, you can help children notice a connection between the number of times 3 appears as an addend and the result of adding that number of 3s (for example, $3 + 3 = 6$ means that adding two 3s equals 6). If you are introducing multiplication, tasks such as Saving for a Bicycle are a good way to contextualize this concept so that children can build their understanding of multiplication as repeated addition while also developing their understanding of functional relationships.

To make this activity more concrete for young children, set up a bank in your class where children deposit play money each week. Over time, the class can keep track of the amount saved using a function table as in Figure 4–14. As your students experience saving the money and recording the

---

Saving for a Bicycle

Every week Mark's Dad gives him $3 for helping with chores around the house. Mark is saving his money to buy a bicycle. How much money has he saved after two weeks? Three weeks? Four weeks? How much money has he saved after twenty weeks? If the bike costs $60, how many weeks will it take to have enough money for the bicycle?

Figure 4–13 *Saving for a Bicycle Problem*

week number (W)	amount saved (A)
1	3
2	3 + 3 = 6
3	3 + 3 + 3 = 9
4	3 + 3 + 3 + 3 = 12
5	3 + 3 + 3 + 3 + 3 = 15

Figure 4-14 *Function table for Saving for a Bicycle*

amount saved each week, they will begin to build meaning for function tables as well as the two quantities (week number and amount saved) and how they relate. They might describe the relationship in words as "the amount saved is 3 times the number of weeks." Or, if W represents the number of weeks and A represents the amount saved, they might express it in symbols as $A = 3 \times W$ or $A = 3W$.

TEACHER TASK 4.5

Once your students have completed Saving for a Bicycle, give them this modified task:

How would this relationship change if Mark had saved $5 before he began receiving an allowance?

(See Appendix B, page 190, for an explanation.)

It is easy to change the level of difficulty of Saving for a Bicycle by changing the amount of money the child earns each week, or by assuming he already has some money saved. Or, rather than receiving a constant allowance each week (such as $3), the amount of money he earns could increase each week (for example, each week, he could earn one dollar more than he did the previous week). There are numerous ways to adapt the difficulty of this task to a particular grade.

TEACHER TASK 4.6

Find a functional relationship for Saving for a Bicycle if Mark receives an allowance of $4 per week. What if the allowance is $5 a week? How does the function change? (See Appendix B, page 190, for an explanation.)

Build Toward More Complex Functional Relationships

Build toward functional thinking tasks that combine operations in more complex ways. The simple relationships in Counting Dog Eyes or Saving for a Bicycle are *linear* and offer a good starting point for children. One reason for this is that the rate at which linear functions grow (or decay) is constant. In other words, we can describe recursive or growing patterns in data that have a linear relationship in ways such as "add two every time" (Counting Dog Eyes—see Figure 3–3, page 34) or "add 3 every time" (Trapezoid Table Problem—see Figure 3–6, page 36), where the constant value being added each time depends on the relationship in the data.

In a more formal sense, linear relationships between two variables are those for which the dependent variable can be expressed as some (real)[2] number times the independent variable plus a (real) number. This relationship can be written symbolically as $y = ax + b$, where a and b represent fixed numbers in the function,[3] x represents the independent variable, and y represents the dependent variable. For example, with Counting Dog Eyes the relationship can be expressed as $E = 2D$, where E represents the number of eyes (dependent variable) and D the number of dogs (independent variable). In this case, E is 2 times D plus the number 0, so the value of a is 2 and the value of b is 0.

Tasks like the Trapezoid Table Problem (Figure 3–6, page 36) and Cutting String (Figure 3–19, page 50) also have linear relationships. For example, in the Trapezoid Table Problem the function describing the relationship between the number of tables and number of people seated is $P = 3t + 2$. In this case, P, the number of people seated, is 3 times t, the number of tables, plus the number 2. Thus, the value of a is 3 and the value of b is 2.

On the other hand, tasks such as the Handshake Problem, Growing Snake, or Growing Caterpillar involve more complex relationships known as

---

[2]While the functional relationships in this book are based on real number values, the tasks are designed to have input values that are natural numbers.

[3]The symbols a and b play a very different role than that of x and y. In particular, a and b are specific (constant) numbers that do not change for a particular function. However, x and y are variables that can take on a range of values for a particular function.

quadratic functions. Quadratic functions can be expressed in symbols as $y = ax^2 + bx + c$, where a, b, and c are (real) numbers, a is never 0, x is the independent variable, and y is the dependent variable.[4] For example, with Growing Snake the number of body parts was given by $n \times n + 1$, or $n^2 + 1$. In this example, $a = 1$, $b = 0$, and $c = 1$. With the Handshake Problem, the total number of handshakes for a group with n people could be expressed as $\frac{n \times (n - 1)}{2}$, or $\frac{1}{2} n^2 - \frac{1}{2} n$. In this case, $a = \frac{1}{2}$, $b = -\frac{1}{2}$, and $c = 0$.

Because quadratic relationships can be more difficult for children to identify (unlike linear relationships, their growing patterns are not constant), children might rely solely on guessing techniques to find the function rule. However, well-chosen hints from the teacher can guide children to analyze patterns in the data or to reason from the structure or context of the problem in order to identify a functional relationship. Let's consider again Angela's reflection on how her students solved Growing Snake (see Chapter 3, page 42). We don't know how Callie arrived at the function $n \times n + 1$ or why she thought it might be correct. She might have guessed the rule through trial and error and tested particular function values to see if the relationship was consistent with what she observed in the snake drawings. But she might have developed a more general argument by reasoning about the structure of the problem in order to model the situation.

Let's think about what this might mean. If you examine the number of body parts excluding the head of the snake, you will notice that on Day 1 there is 1 body part, on Day 2 there are 4 body parts, and on Day 3 there are 9 body parts. Children who have experience with square numbers will recognize this pattern in the sequence 1, 4, 9. . . . (They might observe other valid patterns as well.) The *total* number of body parts on an arbitrary day, then, is the square number corresponding to that day plus 1 for the head of the snake. The head of the snake always contributes one body part to the total number of body parts, regardless of the number of days. So, on Day 2 the total number of body parts is $2^2 + 1$, on Day 3 it is $3^2 + 1$, and so forth. For Day n, the total number of body parts is $n^2 + 1$, or as Callie described it, $n \times n + 1$.

Linear and quadratic functions are just two types of functional relationships children might begin to explore. Another type is an *exponential function*. In order to understand exponential functions, let's first look at an example. A good task involving exponential functions is Folding Paper (see Figure 4–15; see also Appendix A, page 168, for a solution).

---

[4]The notation x^2 means $x \times x$.

Folding Paper

Materials: One piece of plain white paper per student or group

1. Fold your paper in half. Open the paper and count how many regions this created on your piece of paper (see figure).

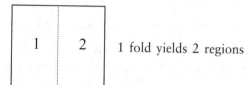

1 fold yields 2 regions

2. Refold the paper, then fold it in half again. How many regions do you now have on your piece of paper?

3. Repeat this, folding the paper in half a third time. Count the number of regions you now have on your paper.

4. Organize your data in a table. Do you notice a relationship between the number of folds and the number of regions? How would you describe the pattern? Write it in words or symbols.

5. Without folding the paper, if you continued this process until you folded your original piece of paper 10 times, how many regions would this create?

Figure 4–15 *Folding Paper Problem*

When fourth-grade teacher Lorraine Gagne gave her students Folding Paper to solve, she had them work in pairs to find the number of regions for up to 5 folds and organize their data in some way. All of her students used function tables to do this. She wrote about their thinking when she asked them to find the number of regions for 10 folds without folding the paper:

> Knowing that there was much more to the problem, I asked the students to figure out how many regions there would be if we had 10 folds. I suggested that they think about what happened to the regions each time they folded the paper. Dana yelled out, "It[5] doubles each

[5] When discussing this task with your students, care should be taken regarding what is being referenced by "it." Note that with Counting Dog Eyes, children might describe the relationship as "It doubles." In this case, "it" refers to the independent variable (the number of dogs) as the quantity being doubled. However, with Dana's observation "It doubles each time," "it" refers to the number of regions (dependent variable). In the first case (Counting Dog Eyes), the language describes a correspondence relationship, while in the second case (Folding Paper) it describes a recursive relationship.

no. of folds	no. of regions
1	2 1×2
2	4 $1 \times 2 \times 2$
3	8 $1 \times 2 \times 2 \times 2$
4	16 $1 \times 2 \times 2 \times 2 \times 2$
5	32 $1 \times 2 \times 2 \times 2 \times 2 \times 2$

Figure 4–16 *Function table for Folding Paper*

time." I demonstrated one fold and wrote 1×2 on the chart next to fold one. Then I asked, "What will happen when I fold the paper again?" They all knew it would double. I reminded the students that we already had 1×2 and asked them to come up with a number sentence to represent the second fold. One of the students said $1 \times 2 \times 2$. I wrote this next to fold 2. We went right down the chart multiplying what we already had by 2. Our class chart now looked like this (see Figure 4–16).

At this point, I figured it would be a good opportunity to introduce exponents and review the multiplication properties of 1. I asked the students what happens when you multiply by 1. All of the students knew that when you multiply by 1 you get that number. (We had previously written conjectures on this topic.) I asked them if we had to multiply by 1, and they realized that the 1 was unnecessary in our problems. I crossed out the 1s, leaving the 2s in place.

Suddenly Allison couldn't contain herself any longer. She yelled out, "Mrs. Gagne, I can figure out how many regions for 10 folds." I asked her to let us in on her secret. She had recognized that you multiplied 2 by itself the number of times you folded the paper. Excitement filled the air as students lit up like light bulbs. I then gave the students time to figure out how many regions for 10 folds with the use of calculators to save time. I also briefly introduced exponents. Of course, I had to tell the students that I didn't learn about exponents until I was in high school. This made them all feel confident and excited.

Lorraine addressed a lot of important mathematical ideas with this task. As she pointed out:

> This turned out to be a valuable lesson. Students were introduced to exponents and functions that were not linear or quadratic, they recognized patterns, revisited the identity property of multiplication, gained experience in using a calculator (this became a lesson in itself), and used visuals to aid learning.

Moreover, students explored these issues in the context of a task of discovery and inquiry that engaged their thinking. For example, Folding Paper provided a novel way to introduce exponents. Rather than just defining the term and giving examples, Lorraine introduced exponents in a context in which children were making mathematical meaning.

To help students find a pattern, she made another important instructional choice: In a manner similar to leaving sums in their unexecuted form, Lorraine wrote products in unexecuted form (for example, $8 = 2 \times 2 \times 2$). This was a critical move that helped Allison see the functional relationship. It is also a reminder that computations can sometimes hide important information. Be able to guide your students' thinking so that arithmetic doesn't hinder the algebra!

Finally, although Lorraine's students described the relationship in words, students in other (upper) elementary grades were able to express it in symbols (using their own choice of literals) as $r = 2^f$, where f represented the number of folds and r represented the number of regions.

In general, a simple exponential function can be expressed in symbols as $y = a^x$, where x is the independent variable, y is the dependent variable, and a is a specific (constant) number greater than zero. Depending on the task, exponential functions can be more complex than linear or quadratic functions. As such, in elementary grades, task designs are best rooted in concrete situations (such as folding paper) that use values for the independent and dependent variables (or, input and output) that are meaningful to children. In later grades, students will explore more complicated types of exponential functions that can take on a broader range of values. Although children will need experience with multiplication and multiplicative reasoning in order to describe these functional relationships, younger children can begin an exploration of exponential functions by focusing on generating and organizing data and looking for recursive patterns.

TEACHER TASK 4·7

Construct the graphs of a linear function, a quadratic function, and an exponential function. For example, you might construct the graphs of the functions from the Trapezoid Table Problem, Growing Caterpillar, and Folding Paper. How do their graphs compare? What do you notice about their similarities and differences? Find a recursive pattern in each function. Based on this pattern, what can you say about the rate at which each graph grows? (See Appendix B, page 191 for an explanation.)

Conclusion

We have considered only three types of functions: linear, quadratic, and exponential. The functions we look at in this book are purposely selected because they have relatively simple relationships that children can analyze and identify by techniques such as analyzing number patterns or reasoning from the context or structure of the problem. The tasks are also based on concrete situations for which the function values typically involve simple whole numbers[6] (for example, the number of people in a group and the corresponding number of handshakes are both quantities that can have only whole-number values).

However, in general, functions can be complicated to express and analyze, and the values of the independent and dependent variables can be quite messy. Indeed, much more could be said about these and other types of functional relationships, what their general forms look like, how they each behave, how their graphs are different, how their recursive patterns differ, and so forth. Some functions have very complicated forms for which methods of identification discussed here, such as analyzing number patterns or reasoning from a problem context, fail. Moreover, for some functions—particularly those that model real-world, often messy, data—it might be impossible to identify an exact relationship between quantities. In this case, more sophisticated computational methods can be used to find functions that approximate the relationship in data.

A formal discussion of functional thinking is not only beyond the scope of this book, but also the intent of early algebra. The point of early algebra

---

[6]The only exception to this is the Spinner Problem, which has fractional output values for the dependent variable.

is not for children to develop a rigorous knowledge of different types of functions in elementary grades. They are not expected to know the general, symbolic forms of different types of functions (for example, $y = ax^2 + bx + c$) given here. They are not expected to use complicated numbers that would detract from their ability to focus on relationships in data. Instead, the aim of this chapter is to help you find ways to integrate functional thinking into your daily instruction and, as part of that, be attentive to the kind of relationship your function involves, its level of complexity, and how to scaffold children's thinking so that they can handle increasingly complex functions. As children learn more advanced mathematics in later grades, they will encounter these and other types of functions through more formal studies.

The following key points summarize the ideas discussed in this chapter for how to develop functional thinking tasks and scaffold children's thinking about these tasks in instruction:

- Think of an arithmetic question that counts some quantity per unit (for example, the number of eyes per dog).

- Vary a task parameter (for example, the number of dogs) to create a set of questions that looks at how a quantity is changing. For example, if you vary the number of dogs, you might generate a set of questions such as How many eyes for one dog? Two dogs? Three dogs? One hundred dogs?

- Use numbers algebraically. Choose the *highest value* of the parameter you vary to be large enough so that children can't solve the task using arithmetic skills and, instead, must attend to the underlying structure and relationship in the task in order to solve it. For example, with Counting Dog Eyes, you might ask children in later elementary grades to find the number of eyes for 100 dogs. One hundred is small enough to be understandable, but large enough that children would not use arithmetic to solve the task. For children in the early elementary grades, a number as low as 10 might be sufficient.

- Guide children to look for a function that describes a relationship between two quantities (for example, the number of dogs and the number of dog eyes). Depending on the age and experience of your students, they might instead identify a recursive pattern.

- For some tasks, it can be helpful to leave number sentences in unexecuted form as an alternative way to generalize a relationship between quantities. The structure of a number sentence used to find a quantity (such as the number of handshakes in a group of 4 children) contains important information about patterns in the data. Computing the number sentence hides this information.

▪ Describe the relationship in words or symbols. Encourage children to use their natural language, particularly if they have had few experiences with early algebra. Scaffold their thinking so that their language becomes more symbolic over time.

▪ If possible, incorporate important mathematical concepts from geometry, probability, measurement, and so forth—concepts other than those in arithmetic—to broaden students' opportunity for algebraic thinking.

▪ Vary the problem design to create a *family* of functional thinking tasks (e.g., Generalizing the String Problem).

▪ Start with tasks that have simple functional relationships. Linear functions (such as those found in Counting Dog Eyes, Saving for a Bicycle, Cutting String, and the Trapezoid Table Problem) can be good starting points.

▪ Build toward more complex functional relationships such as quadratic and exponential. Tasks like the Handshake Problem, Growing Caterpillar, and Folding Paper are good examples of tasks you might use with your students.

Remember that at different grade levels children will focus on different mathematical features of a task. While children in the early elementary grades might not be able to find a functional relationship for a particular task, they are learning equally important age-appropriate concepts such as finding and organizing data, developing an understanding of dependent quantities by constructing function tables, or even finding recursive patterns.

CHAPTER 5

What About Children's Arithmetic Skills?

The purpose of computation is insight, not numbers.

—Richard W. Hamming

At this point, you might be wondering how children will learn the arithmetic concepts you are expected to teach. As described earlier, algebraic thinking is not an add-on to your curriculum. It is instead a way to rethink what you already teach so that it's deeper, richer, and more powerful for students. But, in spite of these reassurances, you might still be asking yourself, "Will my students learn their facts?" Chapter 2 focused on finding the algebra in arithmetic. In this chapter, we look at finding the *arithmetic* in *algebra*.

I know children are learning their facts through [algebraic thinking] problems. Even though it is disguised, students are doing multiplication, addition, division, and subtraction every time they do one of these problems. And, because the focus is not on them knowing their facts fast and automatically, it seems to come to them.

Angela Gardiner, third-grade teacher

Finding the Arithmetic in Algebra

This chapter draws further on classroom stories and teachers' reflections to show that early algebra—through functional thinking and generalized arithmetic—*does* help children learn their facts (and other arithmetic skills and concepts) and, perhaps more important, learn them *in context*. Children strengthen their arithmetic knowledge as they engage in more advanced mathematical (algebraic) thinking through contexts that are richer and more meaningful than computational exercises alone. In particular, early algebra provides opportunities for practicing computations, for working with operations, and for exploring important arithmetic ideas such as counting on all in novel and more mathematically complex situations. Contextualizing the arithmetic in algebraic thinking helps develop children's arithmetic understanding because their calculations are purposeful, related to one another, and related to other knowledge that they are building.

> I have noticed that, without the pressure, students are performing better [on arithmetic skills]. Students who didn't know their number facts are now using multiplication to solve the problems I am giving them. They know that they must learn multiplication if they want to solve these problems.
>
> *Angela Gardiner, third-grade teacher*

? THINK ABOUT IT 5.1

What would you think about literacy instruction if the goal was primarily for students to learn to spell? Would you agree that simply teaching children to spell provides them with the necessary skills to write in various literary genres or read and critique the works of others? In a similar way, mathematics instruction that focuses only on arithmetic facts, skills, and procedures—while these are important—leaves a big void in developing children's mathematical understanding.

Finding Arithmetic in the Handshake Problem

Algebraic thinking tasks are an important way for children to strengthen arithmetic skills and understanding. One of the arithmetic concepts that children encounter is the notion of counting on. Children who are not able to count on will continue to recount a set of objects. For example, if a child has determined a set to contain 5 objects and 3 more objects are added to the set, then to determine the new total amount, he will re-count the original 5 objects (as well as the 3 newly added objects) rather than counting on from 5.

Children in June Soares' class tackled this arithmetic concept when solving the Handshake Problem. When an additional person was added to a group shaking hands, some children began recounting handshakes. When June challenged this, they realized that they did not need to re-count handshakes that had already been counted. After children found the number of handshakes for a group of 8 people, she asked them for the number of handshakes in a group of 12. Zolan and Jackson explained their solution:

ZOLAN: We put 11, 10, 9, 8 . . . (*voice trails off*). You don't need to add 1 through 7 over again (*students had already computed the sum for the number sentence 1 + 2 + 3 + 4 + 5 + 6 + 7 as the number of handshakes for a group of 8 people*).

JACKSON: All you have to do is put 11, 10, 9, 8 on top of all the numbers we had (*referring to the computed sum of 1 + 2 + 3 + 4 + 5 + 6 + 7*).

As these students shared their insights about counting on with the class, it challenged other students' understanding of counting.

But this concept can be addressed in earlier grades as well. Fran Vincent described how her first-grade students worked with counting on in the context of the Handshake Problem. After she and the class constructed a T-chart recording the number of handshakes for 1, 2, 3, 4, 5, 6, and 7 people in a group, she asked how to find the number of handshakes for a group of 8 people:

"How much will 8 people's handshakes go up by?" "7" was an immediate response from one of my students. Then I probed further, "If it goes up by 7 more, how many handshakes will 8 people make?" Three students answered together, "28." "Fabulous, how did you get the answer?" "I counted on," one girl stated. "Good, let's do it together, here we go. Pull down the 21 and count on 7 more. I pulled down my hand and began, "21, 22, 23, 24, 25, 26, 27, 28." As I said it I used my fingers to add the seven more. More children seemed to understand.

The act of shaking hands also requires children to understand the correspondence between a collection of counted handshakes and the numeral representing it, such as identifying four shakes as 4 (Blanton and Kaput 2004). While this was not difficult for June's third graders, it is relevant for earlier grades, where children are learning counting actions. The

Principles and Standards for School Mathematics (NCTM 2000) says that children in grades pre-K through two should be able to "connect number words and numerals to the quantities they represent, using various physical models and representations" and "recognize 'how many' in sets of objects" (78). Tasks such as the Handshake Problem provide mathematically interesting contexts in which children can explore these ideas.

The *Principles and Standards for School Mathematics* also states that children in grades three through five should "understand and use properties of operations" (such as the commutative and associative properties of addition), and "develop fluency with basic number combinations . . . and use these combinations to mentally compute related problems such as 30×50" (148). It defines computational fluency as "having efficient and accurate methods for computing" (152). Algebraic thinking tasks provide contexts in which children can practice efficient counting strategies and apply properties of operations. For example, the lengthy number sentence students formed to determine the number of handshakes for a group of 20 (0 + 1 + 2 + 3 + 4 + 5 + 6 + 7 + 8 + 9 + 10 + 11 + 12 + 13 + 14 + 15 + 16 + 17 + 18 + 19) prompted students, with June's encouragement, to look for a more efficient strategy for computing the sum:

JUNE: Is there a way that we can change the order of these numbers and make them easier to add up?

ANTHONY: You can take the zero and put it, you can change it around by putting the 19 where the zero was and that would be easier.

JUNE: Can I do this? If I do this, 19 + 0 . . .

JACKSON: That equals 19.

JUNE: What else could I do?

ZOLAN: You could do 18 + 1.

MICHELLE: What about 17 + 2?

JUNE: What about 17 + 2? Wait a minute. Let me just try this. So I've used those two (*19, 18*) and these two numbers (*0, 1*) *June draw lines on the board connecting 19 to 0 and 18 to 1. [See Figure 5–1.]* Let me see . . . 17 + 2. Okay. These are pairs aren't they? How many pairs of

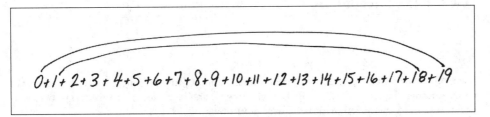

Figure 5–1 *June's drawing of the number pairs students formed*

numbers do you think we're going to be able to make out of these 20 numbers? Anthony, how many do you think we are going to make?

ANTHONY: Ten.

JUNE: Why?

ANTHONY: Because you need to get 1 from each side.

JUNE: Let's see if we do make 10 pairs of numbers.

ZOLAN: Each one (*pair*) is equal to 19.

After they had established that there would be 10 pairs of numbers, the sum of each being 19, June said, "Now I've got to add up all these 19s. What is this?

ZOLAN: Repeated addition. You could do times.

JUNE: I could do times?

ZOLAN: Nineteen times 10. One hundred and ninety.

All of these processes—counting on, commuting and reassociating numbers, counting handshakes for groups of various sizes, and seeing repeated addition as multiplication—occurred in a more complex algebraic task in which students explored relationships and properties of numbers. In other words, arithmetic was an integral part of solving the Handshake Problem. At the same time, the task provided a fun and engaging way for children to practice arithmetic skills and refine their arithmetic understanding.

In all of these activities, computational skills are needed to arrive at the correct answers. But the computation just isn't the entire focus of the activity. The difference is now students are having fun and learning to think for themselves rather than focusing on skills.

Judy Jennings, fourth-grade teacher

But these experiences are not unique to the Handshake Problem. In general, functional thinking tasks[1] are important ways your students can develop facility with number and operation. The next section illustrates how these connections can occur in earlier grades.

---

[1]Generalized arithmetic is equally important as a domain for building children's arithmetic understanding. Functional thinking is highlighted here because the connections between arithmetic and generalized arithmetic are more obvious.

TEACHER TASK 5.1

Identify ways in which tasks used in this book (or other early algebra tasks that you know about) give children an opportunity to think about counting on; practice skip-counting; connect number words to the numerals they represent; model situations that entail addition, subtraction, multiplication, and division; explore properties of operations (e.g., commutativity, associativity); develop efficient computational strategies, and so forth.

Implications for Earlier Grades

Children in earlier elementary grades (pre-K–2) can reasonably be expected to reach different levels of understanding in early algebra tasks than children in grades three through five. Different issues move to the foreground at different ages, and as children mature they are able to handle more complex components of a task.

A particular advantage of algebraic thinking tasks in the earlier grades is that they provide opportunities to strengthen early number concepts, concepts that older children have already mastered. The *Principles and Standards for School Mathematics* (NCTM 2000) states, "during the early years (pre-K–2) teachers must help students strengthen their sense of number, moving from the initial development of basic counting techniques to more-sophisticated understandings of the size of numbers, number relationships, patterns, operations and place value" (79).

One of the ways children develop facility with number and number relationships is through skip-counting, and functional thinking tasks provide rich opportunities to practice this. First-grade teacher Julie Boardman describes her students' experiences with skip-counting with the Squares and Vertices Problem (see Figure 3–14, page 44):

My students have not had much exposure to skip-counting by threes. They have had opportunities with twos, fives, and tens, and these numbers are much more familiar to them. I pointed to the first square (Figure 1 in Figure 3–14) and said, "There are four vertices here for this first square. There are seven vertices here on these two squares (Figure 2 in Figure 3–14). To get from four to seven, how many do you have to add on?" I told them to try by counting on from four to seven. Finally, Jamal said, "Three." I said, "Okay, great! You need three more added to four to get to seven. Now what do you notice about going from seven to ten?" For some reason, they still seemed to have a hard time realizing that ten is three away from seven. I had to ask probing questions, but we eventually found it out. I wanted to do the last comparison between Figures 3 and 4 just so they would start to see the relationship forming.

When I asked what they noticed about the numbers ten and thirteen, Jamal immediately replied, "Thirteen is three more than ten." I was not sure if he had actually counted this, or if he was relying on what he saw from four to seven, and seven to ten (the notion of three more each time). I said to Jamal, "Can you justify your answer? Explain how you got three." He said, "Every time you get one more number, you get three more than that each time." I said, "Okay, and thirteen is three more than ten?" Jamal replied, "Yes." I said, "We can also figure it out by counting on. I don't need to repeat all the numbers up to ten. I can just say, 'Ten (holding up fingers for the rest) eleven, twelve, thirteen.' That's three more!"

Skip-counting is important for algebraic thinking because it focuses on relationships in numbers. Building the notion of repeating an operation (such as adding 3 repeatedly) to get successive values can help children find recursive patterns. Furthermore, Jamal extended the recursive pattern to a co-varying relationship by connecting the act of repeatedly adding 3 to a 1-unit increase in the figure number ("Every time you get one more number, you get 3 more than that each time").

From an arithmetic perspective, the Squares and Vertices problem gave children in Julie's class an opportunity to think about—and practice—skip-counting by 3. This in itself is an important means for developing computational fluency, for understanding the relative positions of and relationships between numbers, and for learning to count with understanding (NCTM 2000). It is an added benefit that children were able to practice these arithmetic skills in a context that was purposeful, interesting, and algebraic.

TEACHER TASK 5.2

What skip-counting number are you focusing on in your instruction? Design a functional thinking task that helps your children practice skip-counting a particular number. For example, Counting Dog Eyes is a good task for skip-counting by 2, while Counting Eyes and Tails helps children practice skip-counting by 3.

There are other important insights we can glean from this case. First, Julie also used this task to develop children's notion of counting on ("I told them to try by counting on from four to seven"; "We can also figure it out by counting on. I don't need to repeat all the numbers up to ten. I can just say, 'Ten (holding up fingers for the rest) eleven, twelve, thirteen.' That's three more!").

Moreover, it is worth pointing out that this task (and many other functional thinking tasks) does not address just arithmetic and algebra. Like the Tower Problem or the Trapezoid Table Problem, it also makes important connections to geometry. In particular, it gives children an opportunity to look for patterns in geometric figures and to generate unknown geometric figures (as Julie's children later did). It also exposes children to new vocabulary terms (for example, *vertex*, *vertices*) and to opportunities to refine their understanding of geometric objects or concepts (For example, is a square a rectangle? Is a rectangle a square? How are they alike or different?). Based on your knowledge of your own students' understanding and the grade level you teach, you can draw out the relevant geometric (and arithmetic) issues inherent in these tasks.

TEACHER TASK 5.3

Select an early algebra task and identify the arithmetic skills and concepts it uses that are relevant to the grade you teach. Compare your students' *interest* in solving this early algebra task to an arithmetic task that addresses these same skills or concepts.

Conclusion

Given the hectic pace of today's classrooms, the advantage of early algebra is that children can do many important things at once, including building number sense, practicing number facts, and building and recognizing patterns to model situations. It can provide practice of arithmetic skills in a context that intrigues students and that avoids the mindlessness of computational worksheets.

Arithmetic understanding, including the skills and procedures that go along with it, are an essential part of elementary grades mathematics and a necessary part of thinking algebraically. As such, it is important to remember that early algebra does not ignore a computational agenda for classrooms, but, rather, enlarges that agenda by integrating the learning of basic skills and number sense into deeper mathematical understandings (Kaput and Blanton 2005).

Changing *How* I Teach

When I look back at the way I had been teaching math, I know now that I was not a great math teacher. I remember standing in front of the class teaching math, and it was so unfulfilling I would often not want to teach it. If I skipped math some days, I didn't care. I was not making my students think. I was making them memorize strategies to subtract, add, and multiply. I wanted them to know their facts fast and automatically.

I would often stand in front of my students and teach them what was important for them to learn. There were many discussions in my classroom, but I did not allow the students to run or drive the discussion. It was my job to do that. I often allowed my students to run discussions when it came to literacy or science, but with math I just never thought of it.

I have now changed how I run my classroom. It is no longer about me, but about students. My math lessons are now student driven. My room also looks different and the writing that goes on my board when doing a lesson also looks very different. I now even have a board dedicated to math conjectures.

—Angela Gardiner, third-grade teacher

As with Angela, building a classroom where children think algebraically might change some (or many!) of the teaching practices you currently use. In fact, an important aspect of early algebra is that tasks and curriculum alone are not enough—your expertise as a teacher is essential in the development of children's algebraic thinking. This section looks at practices that support children's thinking, including questioning strategies you might use, ways of listening to children's ideas to find and exploit algebra opportunities, ways to help children build and connect multiple representations of their thinking, and ways to help children generalize their mathematical ideas by forming and testing mathematical conjectures. As you read this section, compare your current practice with the ideas contained here. Look at the similarities and the differences, and develop a plan for how you might make changes.

CHAPTER 6

Teaching Practices That Develop Children's Algebraic Thinking Skills

Algebraic thinking tasks alone will not give students the skills they need to reason algebraically. *How these tasks are used in instruction is equally important.*

In the discussion on the meanings children give the symbol = (Chapter 2), we saw that tasks by themselves can lead to unintended learning that can even hinder students' algebraic thinking. On the other hand, a simple task like $9 + 3 = \square + 4$ can be a source of thoughtful classroom investigation if the teacher uses it to challenge students' understanding of equality. But what would this instruction look like? What would the teacher's role be? What would students' roles be? How can a teacher give a task more algebraic meaning for children? This chapter tries to unearth some of these skills and discuss specific ways for teachers to develop algebraic thinking in the classroom.

Represent, Question, Listen, Generalize

Classroom instruction that supports children's algebraic thinking is marked by rich conversation in which children make and explore mathematical conjectures, build arguments to establish or refute these conjectures, and treat established conjectures (generalizations) as important pieces of shared classroom knowledge. Moreover, this type of instruction treats these processes as a *regular* part of classroom activity, not an occasional enrichment to routines such as practicing arithmetic skills and procedures. In other words, algebraic thinking is a habit of mind that students acquire through instruction that builds regular, sustained opportunities to think about, describe, and justify general relationships in arithmetic, geometry, and so on. There are four important instructional goals for you to keep in mind as you help children think algebraically:

- Represent: Provide multiple ways for children to systematically represent algebraic situations.

- Question: Ask questions that encourage children to think algebraically.

- Listen: Listen to and build on children's thinking.

- Generalize: Help children develop and justify their own generalizations.

Let's turn our attention to what these goals entail and what they might look like in instruction.

Represent: Provide Multiple Ways to Represent Algebraic Situations

> As I walk around to each group, students are doing something different to solve the problem. Some groups are drawing pictures, some are using words and symbols, while others still are working on charts and graphs. It is quite refreshing to see my class take ownership of their learning.
>
> *Lina Fidalgo, fourth-grade teacher*

Elementary teachers are being asked to think creatively and flexibly about the types of representations that will make mathematics meaningful in their classrooms. The *Principles and Standards for School Mathematics* (NCTM 2000) notes, "a major responsibility of teachers is to create a learning environment in which students' use of multiple representations is encouraged" (139). Its Representation Standard states that instruction should enable all children to:

1. create and use representations to organize, record, and communicate mathematical ideas;

2. select, apply, and translate among mathematical representations to solve problems; and

3. use representations to model and interpret physical, social, and mathematical phenomena. (67)

Figure 6–1 *Representations for reasoning about even and odd sums*

The term *representation* refers to both the *process* of representing an idea and the *product*, or result, of that process (NCTM 2000). For instance, to explore whether the sum of an even number and an odd number is even or odd, children may represent their thinking using number sentences consisting of specific even and odd numbers, or with pictures of squares, paired together, from a collection of squares (see Figure 6–1). Either is a representation of the *process* of reasoning about the sum of an even number and an odd number. Once children determine that the sum will always be odd, they may represent this *product* in words as "the sum of an even number and odd number is always odd," or they might use the same number sentences or pictures to represent the result—or product—of their thinking.

Representations can take many forms. They may involve words, symbols, pictures, diagrams, tables, or graphs. With functional thinking, such as in the task Counting Dog Eyes, children might represent the relationship in words ("the number of eyes is twice the number of dogs"), symbols ($E = 2D$), tables (see Figure 3–1, page 33), or graphs (see Figure 3–17, page 47). Representations may be given in oral, written, or tactile forms. The choice

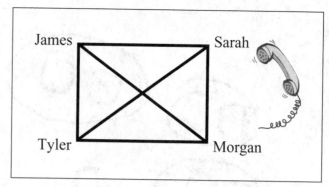

Figure 6–2 *Line segment diagram tracking phone
calls between four people*

of representation varies by both grade level and the mathematical experience
of the learner. Some children need access to handheld manipulatives, such as
pattern blocks, candies, or paper cutouts. Some need to physically act out a
process, such as shaking hands with their friends to count handshakes in a
group. Some are content to make drawings on paper, such as diagrams where
line segments track phone calls among a group of people (see Figure 6–2).

Typically, the younger the child, the more physical or concrete the representations need to be. For the Outfit Problem (see Figure 6–3; see also
Appendix A, page 177, for a solution), first-grade teacher Gail Sowersby
created construction paper cutouts of different-colored shirts and pants that
students could place on chart paper at the front of the room. Her young
students needed to physically see and manipulate the different outfits by
pairing the construction-paper cutouts.

Outfit Problem

1. If you have 2 shirts and 3 pairs of pants, how many different
   outfits* can you make? Show how you got your solution.
2. How many outfits will there be if you have 3 shirts (and 3 pants)?
   What if you have 4 shirts? Five shirts? Organize your data in a
   table. Do you see a relationship? Describe it in words or symbols.

Based on your relationship, predict how many outfits there will be if
you have 20 shirts (and 3 pairs of pants).

Ms. Sowersby's First-Grade Outfit Problem: If you have 1 shirt and
2 pairs of pants, how many outfits can you make? What if you have
2 shirts? Three shirts?

*Assume an outfit consists of 1 shirt and 1 pair of pants.

Figure 6–3 *Outfit Problem*

Maggie	Melissa and Sandra	Dana
red shirt, blue pants	red, blue	RS, BP

Figure 6–4 *Representations of outfits*

When children have multiple ways to represent an idea, they can choose representations that are intrinsically meaningful to them. As a result, they are more likely to be successful with the task at hand. Laura Hunt describes how her third-grade students, working in small groups to solve the Outfit Problem, searched for representations that were convincing to them:

Four children, who happened to be distributed among different groups, began to organize their findings after working with the problem for several minutes. For each outfit combination, Maggie wrote the color of the piece of clothing, as well as the piece of clothing's name. Melissa and Sandra simply wrote each different color combination, eliminating any reference to the piece of clothing, while Dana wrote the initial for each color followed by an initial for the piece of clothing it represented (see Figure 6–4).

Many students used an index finger to map out . . . the various outfits that could be made. Students who were using their fingers . . . were having a hard time convincing their tablemates that they had arrived at all the possible combinations.

Some students . . . drew lines to represent the different outfit combinations. Colon actually used different-colored pencils for each of the lines he used to represent the different outfits.

Several students asked if they could color the outfits. It appeared to me that these students had initially looked to others in the group to solve the problem . . . and now they needed proof for themselves.

After about fifteen minutes of small group work, Laura asked children to share at the board the different ways they represented finding all the outfits; the class discussed whether each representation was convincing. From an instructional perspective, several things are significant here:

■ Children were encouraged to choose representations that were meaningful to them.

■ Children were given time to develop these representations as they explored the Outfit Problem.

■ Children were encouraged to share and critique different representations.

These processes support a learning environment where children's use of multiple representations can thrive.

THINK ABOUT IT 6.1

Think about your classroom practice. What is your role when a task such as the Outfit Problem is being solved? What is the role of your students? Who is responsible for representing the ideas? Are children given time and opportunity to represent their own thinking? Are multiple representations shared and discussed publicly?

As you encourage your students to develop and use multiple representations, help them build connections across these representations so that they can transition from concrete to more abstract ways of thinking. "Seeing similarities in the ways to represent different situations is an important step toward abstraction" (NCTM 2000, 138). For first-grade students, this could mean understanding that a square on chart paper represents an actual shirt (see Figure 6–5). With second graders exploring the Handshake Problem (see Figure 4–2, page 59), this might involve making a connection between actually shaking hands and using the initials of a person's name recorded on paper to represent the handshake (see Figure 6–6). For third graders tracking the total number of eyes for a varying number of dogs, this could involve converting function tables into graphs (see

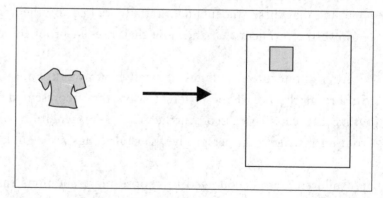

Figure 6–5 *Representations of a shirt*

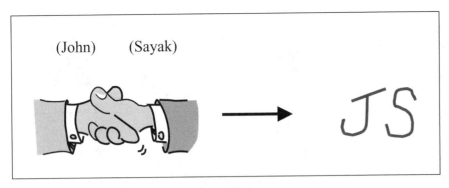

Figure 6–6 *Representation of a handshake*

Figure 6–7). As children develop flexible ways to think about and represent their ideas, they build a richer, more connected understanding of that idea.

Teach Children to Be Organized and Systematic

Elementary teachers can also help children learn to be systematic in how they represent their thinking. On their own, children often record ideas in random, unorganized ways. Teachers can help children learn to organize their data so that mathematical ideas are closer to the surface. For the Outfit Problem, Christie Demers noticed that her third-grade students had drawn pictures of shirts and pairs of pants and were randomly matching them with no clear strategy for keeping track of what combination was already used. She wrote:

> When they kept coming up with different answers each time, I asked them
> if there might be a better way to keep track of the shirts and pants they

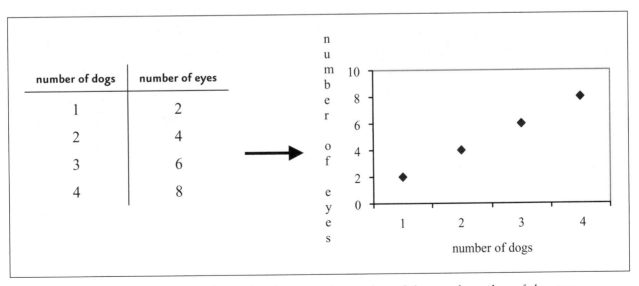

Figure 6–7 *Representations of a relationship between the number of dogs and number of dog eyes*

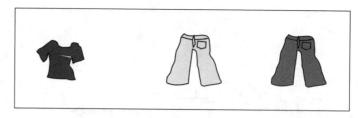

Figure 6–8 *One shirt and two pairs of pants*

were pairing up. One student answered, "Let's match up one pair of pants with all of the shirts, then do the same thing for the other two pairs."

Younger children typically need more explicit scaffolding by the teacher. Cheryl Thadeu, a kindergarten teacher, wrote about the Outfit Problem:

I began by showing children a blue construction paper shirt and two pairs of construction paper pants, one red and one yellow, then asking, "How many different outfits could you make with one shirt and two pairs of pants?" (see Figure 6–8).

After they discussed that an outfit consisted of a shirt and a pair of pants and Cheryl modeled putting an outfit together, she continued:

I made a table on chart paper with one column for shirts and another for pants. I wrote the colors of the shirt and pants that I had used and explained to the children that I was organizing the data this way so we could keep track of the outfits we made and avoid duplicating any outfits (see Figure 6–9).

Then I asked how I could make another *different* outfit using the remaining yellow pants. . . . Nathan responded, "Change the pants," meaning replace the red pants with the yellow pants. I asked the children, "Is this a different outfit?" All agreed that it was. (See Figure 6–10.)

We counted the number of different combinations we were able to make (two). I then said, "Now we're going to add another shirt. How

shirt	pants
blue	red

Figure 6–9 *Table for recording outfits*

shirt	pants
blue	red
blue	yellow

Figure 6-10 *Table for outfits made from one shirt and two pairs of pants*

many outfits could we make with two shirts and two pairs of pants?" (see Figure 6–11).

With help from Cheryl, children were able to make the rest of the outfits quickly and without duplication. She recorded their findings in a table (see Figure 6–12).

Because kindergarten students are only beginning to read and write words and symbols, Cheryl needed to play a more visible role in recording and organizing information in the table. But even at this early age, children can learn to be systematic in how they handle information. The early elementary grades are a critical place for children to learn to use tools and processes that will further their algebraic thinking in later elementary grades. This might involve learning how to organize data in function tables, or what it means to form and test a mathematical conjecture, or how to decompose numbers as a way to think about algebraic properties of number and operation.[1] Thus, while Cheryl's students did not reach a sophisticated generalization about the number of outfits (they conjectured that the total number of outfits increased each time an article of clothing was added), they were beginning to think about how to be systematic in recording and organizing data, the kind of representations that could be used to do this (e.g., tables), and how to publicly talk about their mathematical ideas.

Summary of Ideas for Supporting Use of Multiple Representations

The key points on page 102 summarize how your instruction can help children use multiple representations to think algebraically.

---

[1]For example, children might decompose 3 as 2 + 1 or 1 + 2. This allows them to establish facts such as 1 + 2 = 2 + 1 (since both expressions are equal to 3) and can lead to an exploration of the Commutative Property of Addition.

Figure 6-11 *Two shirts and two pairs of pants*

- Teach children to be organized and systematic in how they represent their thinking.

- Provide children with grade-appropriate manipulatives that can help them make sense of data.

- When possible, provide tasks that allow children to physically act out a process (such as shaking hands).

- Encourage children to share and explain their representations so that all students learn multiple ways to represent or model a problem.

- Build children's flexibility with words, symbols, tables, graphs, and other forms of representation. Although one form of representation might be more meaningful than another to a particular student, encourage children to understand and use all types of representations.

- Give children time to explore different representations and their salient features.

- Help children build connections between concrete and more abstract ways of representing their ideas.

shirt	pants	total
blue	red	
blue	yellow	2
blue	yellow	
blue	red	
green	red	
green	yellow	4

Figure 6-12 *Table showing combinations for one shirt and two pairs of pants and two shirts and two pairs of pants*

Question: Ask Questions That Encourage Children to Think Algebraically

One of the most important things you can do to develop children's algebraic thinking is ask good questions. Classroom stories included in this book show that teaching algebraic thinking is often more about questioning than telling. Asking good questions gives *children* the opportunity to organize their thinking and build mathematical ideas. When a teacher tells children what representation to use or how to symbolize a functional relationship or how to justify a particular conjecture, it lessens the chance for children to develop their own thinking.

Not all questions challenge children's thinking. Think about the kinds of questions you ask your students. What do they require of students? Do they call for students to simply recall number facts or perform computations? Or do they call for students to analyze information, to build arguments, and to explain their reasoning? To help you get started, Figure 6–13 offers several categories of questions that can help give tasks more algebraic meaning for children. Although the questions are stated in general terms, you can modify them to fit your particular task and grade level.

TEACHER TASK 6.1

Make a list of the questions you ask during a particular math lesson. What kinds of questions are they? What do they require of students' thinking? How do your questions compare to the questioning strategies described here?

Listen: Listen to and Build on Children's Thinking

Listening is just as important as questioning. In fact, it has been said that teaching is about those who know being silent so that those who don't know can speak. Often, though, this runs counter to what we feel as teachers. It is instinctive for teachers to help, to tell, to explain. However, listening is critical because it helps you understand children's thinking, and you can use this knowledge to guide your instruction. Also, if you are listening, then children are talking and—more likely—actively engaged in their learning.

Whether students are solving an elaborate task or simply reviewing solutions to homework problems, listen to their ideas, strategies, and reasoning and think about how you can extend their algebraic thinking. An episode in June Soares' third-grade class illustrates how listening to children's thinking can lead to simple, spontaneous ways to include algebraic thinking. While

Questioning Strategies to Build Algebraic Thinking

Ask children to share and explain their ideas (i.e., strategies, representations, conjectures, and reasoning):

- Does anyone have a conjecture* to share?
- How did you model the problem?
- How did you represent your thinking?
- Why did you use this particular representation? How did it help you find the solution?
- What strategy did you use?
- How did you get your solution?
- What does the n stand for in your relationship?

Ask children to compare and contrast their ideas (i.e., strategies, representations, conjectures and reasoning):

- Marta, do you agree with Jack? Why?
- Did anybody get a different solution?
- How are your ideas different?
- Is there a better way to organize the information?
- Would you use a different argument to convince your friends than to convince the teacher? Why?

Ask children to find and describe conjectures about patterns and relationships:

- Do you notice anything that always happens?
- Do you notice anything that is always true?
- How would you describe what is going on in general here?
- Can you describe your pattern (relationship) in words?
- Can you describe your pattern (relationship) in symbols?
- How did you arrive at your pattern (relationship)?

Ask children to justify their conjectures:

- How do you know your conjecture will always be true?
- How do you know your solution will always work?
- How would you convince your friends?
- How could you convince your parents?

Ask children to develop more sophisticated ways of expressing their mathematical ideas:

- How could you describe this relationship using symbols (letters) instead of words?
- How can we represent this unknown quantity? How can we represent this varying quantity? Is there a letter or symbol we can use to represent it that might be easier than writing out the name of the quantity in words?

Figure 6–13 *Questioning strategies to build algebraic thinking*

*For more on conjecturing and justifying, see the section "Components of Building a Generalization" in this chapter. You might want to revisit this set of questioning strategies once you've finished reading about conjecturing and justifying.

reviewing homework solutions of whole-number addition exercises, June asked if the sum 5 + 7 was even or odd. When Tony used arithmetic to answer the question, she challenged his thinking: "How did you get that?" She asked. "I added 5 and 7 and then I looked over there and saw that it was even," Tony explained. (Tony pointed to a list of evens and odds recorded on a chart on the wall. Twelve was on the list of evens.) "What about 45,678 + 85,631? Odd or even?" June asked. "It's odd," Jenna explained. "Why?" June asked. "Because 8 and 1 is even and odd, and even and odd is odd."

June was not only listening, we could say she was listening algebraically. That is, she was listening for children to use arithmetic strategies so that she could create alternative tasks that required algebraic thinking. At this point, her students did not know an arithmetic procedure for finding the sum of 45,678 and 85,631. Using such large numbers[2] required children to look at structural features of the numbers to determine if their sum was even or odd. Jenna was able to answer the question without arithmetic. She looked at the last digit in each number, then to get her result, she used the generalizations that even plus odd is always odd and that the sum would be even or odd based on whether the sum of the last digits was even or odd. Reasoning from structural properties without attending to arithmetic is an important way of thinking algebraically.

TEACHER TASK 6.2

Make an audio recording of one of your math lessons. Play the recording to determine the percentage of time you spend listening to students. How much time do you spend questioning students? How much time do you spend telling students information?

Generalize: Help Children Build Generalizations

The central goal of algebraic thinking is to get children to think about, describe, and justify what is going on *in general* with regard to some mathematical situation. That is, we want children to develop a *generalization*, a statement that describes a general mathematical truth about some set of data. The three instructional goals described so far—*represent*, *question*, and *listen*—are all critical components in helping children build their own generalizations.

---

[2]We refer to this in Chapter 4 as "using numbers algebraically." That is, numbers are treated algebraically because children are attending to their structural properties rather than arithmetic properties.

The Ability to Generalize Builds over Time

The level of generalization that children reach within an activity or task will differ depending on the particular lesson being taught and the grade level. Often, complex ideas need extended periods of time—days, weeks, months, even years—to build in children's thinking. For example, with the Handshake Problem, being able to describe a symbolic relationship between the number of people in a group and the number of handshakes among them can develop over varying amounts of time, based on the age and experience of your students, as children learn to use tools such as function tables to interpret correspondence relationships in data, begin to understand quantities that vary, and develop the mathematical language to symbolize functional relationships.

Don't be discouraged if you find that one algebraic thinking task can consume an entire lesson (or more). Remember that you are asking your students to think at a much deeper level than is required to learn arithmetic skills and procedures. As you observe children begin to develop, explain, and justify complex mathematical ideas, you will find that the payoffs are tremendous.

Components of Building a Generalization[3]

We can characterize the process of building a generalization in the following way (see Figure 6–14):

1. Children are given a mathematical situation to *explore*.

2. They develop a *conjecture*, or mathematical statement that is either true or false.

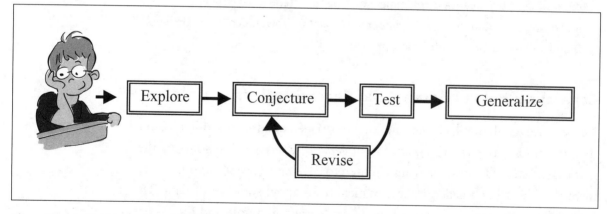

Figure 6–14 *Components of building a generalization*

---

[3]For additional reading on aspects of generalizing, see *Thinking Mathematically: Integrating Arithmetic and Algebra in Elementary School* (Corpenter, Franke, and Levi 2003). The authors provide a detailed treatment of processes such as conjecturing and justifying in the context of generalized arithmetic.

3. They *test* their conjecture to see if it is true or false.

4. If the conjecture is not true, they can *revise* it and test the new conjecture.

5. If the conjecture is confirmed to be true after sufficient evidence is gathered, it becomes a *generalization*.

Explore Algebraic thinking begins with exploration. Give your students opportunity and time to explore mathematical ideas, both with their peers and working alone. Exploring helps children organize their thoughts and decide how to represent or model their thinking. Whether shaking hands with friends, creating different possible outfits for articles of clothing, solving a family of number sentences, gathering and recording information in a function table, or thinking about turnaround facts, children are thinking mathematically when they explore.

Your role as teacher is to give mathematical—algebraic—purpose to the exploration. This can happen through the type of tasks you choose and the questions you ask. For example, you might begin the Handshake Problem by raising the question, "How many handshakes would there be if everyone in your group shook hands once?" (For the complete Handshake Problem, see Figure 4–2, page 59). The mathematical goal here is to find all possible handshakes. Children might explore this by shaking hands with each other, or drawing pictures to represent the different people in the group. Some students might question what it means to shake someone's hand: If Nate shakes hands with Mandy, does it count as a different handshake when Mandy shakes hands with Nate? Some will discuss how to represent a handshake, or how to be systematic in tracking handshakes. All of this calls for children to think (at least implicitly) about questions such as What does it mean for two people to shake hands? What method will help me find all the handshakes? How can I represent the different handshakes? and How will I know that I've gotten all possible handshakes? The purpose of the teacher's question (finding all possible handshakes) shapes the direction of children's thinking. The process of children's thinking, initiated by the teacher's question, is what constitutes the exploration.[4] The point is that the teacher plays a critical role by setting up an issue to explore and allowing children time to explore it.

---

[4] In contrast, questions in which children need only to recall facts or apply algorithms are not exploratory in and of themselves.

Conjecture Generalizing involves making a *conjecture*. A conjecture is a general mathematical statement that is either true or false on a specified domain. For example, the statement "an even number plus an odd number is always even" is a conjecture that is *not* true, since we can find a counterexample: $2 + 3 = 5$ and 5 is not even. On the other hand, the statement "an even number plus an odd number is always odd" is a conjecture that can be shown to be true for all integers. The statement $E = 2D$, where E is the number of dog eyes and D is the number of dogs, is a conjecture about the total number of dog eyes for an arbitrary number of dogs. A conjecture that is true can be called a generalization.

TEACHER TASK 6.3

Think of at least two different ways you could show that the conjecture "Any even number plus any odd number is odd" is true. Which way do you find most convincing? Why?

When children make mathematical conjectures, they have to organize their thoughts to look for a general relationship. Conjecturing requires them to think carefully about many pieces of information simultaneously and how the pieces are connected. Because conjectures are a critical step in building a generalization, children should see conjecturing as an important mathematical activity. One way to start is through conversations with your students about about the meaning of *conjecture* and what it means to make a conjecture. Third-grade teacher Angela Gardiner describes the conversation she had with her students:

I started my lesson by putting these three problems on the board:

$$3 \times 0 = 0$$
$$0 \times 4 = 0$$
$$100 \times 0 = 0$$

I asked my students if these problems were true. They all said yes, confidently. I asked them why the problems were true. The class looked at me a bit puzzled. "What do you mean, why?" asked Simeon. "I mean, why? How do you know that these are all true? Is there a rule that you follow?" I asked. "I know these are all true because anytime you have zero and multiply it by another number, the answer is zero,"[5] Simeon explained. I wrote what Simeon said on the board.

After a similar discussion about a second set of number sentences involving multiplying by 1, Angela continued "Nice job, third graders. What you just did was make conjectures," I told them. "Is a conjecture a rule?" Chandler asked.

"It's very much like a rule, Chandler. The best way I can explain it is when you are working with math and numbers you sometimes see patterns. You sometimes see that every time you do something, there is a certain result. From the data you collect you can make a rule or conjecture and then you must test that rule to see if it works all the time. If it does, you could say that your conjecture is proven," I said.

"I know. We do the same thing in science. As scientists, we make *hypotheses* and those are like conjectures, right?" asked Chandler.

"Yes, exactly, Chandler. If you think of it, scientists use the word *hypothesis*, which means an educated guess that you then have to prove is true. In math, mathematicians make conjectures and then they prove those."

Later in the discussion, Nick asked what makes a number big or small.

"That is a good question, Nick. What do you all think? What makes a number big or small? What rule do you follow?" Angela responded.

"I think a small number is anything below 20," Patrick said.

"I think that a small number is less than 100," added Meaghan.

"So, what do we do? Do we make a conjecture about what a small number is?" asked Nick.

"We could, but could we prove that conjecture?" Angela asked.

"No, because everyone has a different opinion of what a small number is," Callie said.

Through this conversation, Angela helped children see a conjecture as a rule that needed to be tested. It may or may not be true, but it needed to be a statement that could be shown to be true or false. An opinion was not a valid conjecture. She also wrote children's conjectures on the board. Making children's conjectures part of a public record by writing them temporarily on a chalkboard or more permanently on charts hung throughout

[5]Children sometimes use their (re)statement of a conjecture as justification that it is true (see Carpenter, Franke, and Levi 2003).

the room shows that they are valuable mathematical ideas. (Typically, those conjectures displayed permanently are true conjectures, or generalizations.)

Also, because this public record helps children remember the generalizations made, they can more easily build on these ideas. That is, they can use generalizations already established to build justifications for other conjectures. For example, once children establish that the sum of any odd number and any even number is always odd or that the sum of any two odd numbers is always even, they can use these generalizations to explore new conjectures. June Soares wrote about her students' thinking: I asked them, "If we added three odd numbers, what would the sum be?" They figured out that the sum would have to be odd because two odds make an even and when you add odd plus even, you get odd.

A conjecture can be expressed in words or symbols. For example, children might express a conjecture about properties of number and operation in words ("anytime you multiply zero by another number, the answer is zero") or symbols ($0 \times a = 0$). They might conjecture a functional relationship between the number of elephants and elephant legs as "the number of elephant legs is 4 times the number of elephants" or "$L = 4E$" (where L is the number of elephant legs and E is the number of elephants). As discussed earlier, the language children use to express a conjecture will depend in part on their grade level and the richness of their mathematical experiences. The goal is for them to develop more sophisticated mathematical language over time. You will need to adjust your instruction based on your own students and their experiences, but give them the chance to show you how far they can go!

TEACHER TASK 6.4

Introduce the term *conjecture* to your students. Use it in conversations with students so that they become familiar with it.

Test Once children have made a conjecture, they need to test to see if the conjecture is true or false. Not all conjectures are true. Testing involves building a convincing argument, or justification,[6] that the conjecture is either true or false. Let's think about what this means.

---

[6]The term *proof* and its derivatives are purposely not used in this book. While you might use this terminology with your students, its meaning can be ambiguous for a diverse audience. What one might view as proof, another might see as only a strong argument and not a proof in a rigorous, mathematical sense.

A conjecture is false if you can produce one case where it fails to be true. This case is called a *counterexample*. As we just saw, the conjecture "any even number plus any odd number is even" is false, since $2 + 3 = 5$ and 5 is not even. That is, we can find a case where an even number plus an odd number does *not* produce an even number. Note that there are many cases where this conjecture fails to be true: $4 + 9 = 13$; $6 + 5 = 11$; $20 + 13 = 33$; and so on. (In fact, it is always false. Why do you think so?) But to show that a conjecture is false, we only need *one* case where it fails. This is because a conjecture can be true if and only if it is true *for all possible cases on some specified domain*. If it fails for one case on that domain, we say the conjecture is false.

TEACHER TASK 6.5

Have a conversation with your students about the number of cases where the conjecture "any even number plus any odd number is even" fails to be true (there are an infinite number of them). Ask students to think about how many different cases are needed to show the conjecture is false. Introduce them to the notion of a counterexample.

THINK ABOUT IT 6.2

Consider the conjecture "an even number divided by an even number is even." Is it always true? Is it always false? What can you conclude about this? How would you revise the conjecture so that it is always true? (See Appendix C, page 199 for an explanation.)

Give your students experiences with showing a conjecture to be false. False conjectures are easy to construct. One way to do this is to modify a true conjecture so that it no longer holds. For example, simply changing the numbers in a (true) functional relationship will make it a false relationship. A conjecture that the number of dog eyes on D dogs is $3 \times D$ can easily be shown to be false by looking at a particular case: Although children know one dog has 2 eyes, the conjectured function says that one dog has $3 \times 1 = 3$ eyes. It could happen that children conjecture a false relationship to begin with. Use this as an opportunity to explore what it takes to show a conjecture is false.

As another example, suppose that children have established that addition is a commutative operation. That is, the order in which two numbers are added does not matter. We can express the generalization in symbols as $a + b = b + a$, where a and b are (real) numbers. But what if the operation was changed to subtraction? Is the conjecture that $a - b = b - a$, for (real) numbers a and b, true? That is, does the order in which two numbers are subtracted matter? (Note that this introduces negative numbers!) Since we can find a counterexample ($3 - 4 \neq 4 - 3$), we conclude that subtraction is not a commutative operation. In other words, order *does* matter with subtraction. Thus, the conjecture is false and not a generalization.

Sometimes, a conjecture might be true for one set of numbers, but not another. Help children think about the set of numbers for which a conjecture is true and revise their conjectures to reflect this. For example, when children first learn to multiply, they often overgeneralize that "multiplication makes bigger." But this is not always true. In fact, it's easy to challenge this claim when introducing multiplication by thinking about multiplying by zero or one. In later elementary grades, children can use fractions between zero and one to test this claim. In other words, not only is it important for children to investigate *if* a conjecture is true, but also *when* it is true. That is, *for what domain or set of numbers* does the conjecture hold?

TEACHER TASK 6.6

Depending on your grade level, have your students think about the set of numbers (for example, natural numbers, integers, fractions) for which the conjecture "multiplication makes bigger" is true and the set of numbers for which it is false. (See Appendix B, page 193 for an explanation.)

Showing that a conjecture is true ultimately requires building a convincing argument that the claim is true for all possible cases over some domain. But the level of sophistication required to make an argument convincing to someone will vary: The argument that convinces a child will likely not convince a mathematician. In fact, a rigorous mathematical argument—one that a mathematician might make—requires certain tools of logic that young children are not expected to know and understand.

But elementary teachers play an important role in helping children understand the importance of justifying their mathematical ideas and building arguments that are increasingly sophisticated mathematically. Carpenter, Franke, and Levi (2003) describe three levels of arguments or justifications that children make: (1) appealing to an authority figure (a conjecture is true because "the teacher said so"); (2) looking at particular examples or cases; or (3) building generalizable arguments. Let's examine these levels.

Children's justifications will often use simple empirical arguments based on testing a number of specific cases (Carpenter, Franke, and Levi 2003; Schifter in press). For example, to show that the sum of two even numbers is even, children might look at examples of two even numbers added together and base their argument on these results. They might argue that, since 2 + 4 = 6 (even), 2 + 6 = 8 (even), and 4 + 10 = 14 (even), then the sum of any two even numbers will be even. While the number of cases they look at will vary, the essence of their argument is based on looking at whether the conjecture holds for particular examples.

But think about how you might guide your students toward more general arguments. To start with, you can encourage them to use different *types* of numbers in an empirical argument, rather than just a random selection of numbers.

In a conversation with her third-grade students about conjectures, Angela Gardiner asked,

> "We now know what a conjecture is, but how do we prove a conjecture is true? How do we know that any number times 0 equals 0?"
>
> "We would have to try multiplying a lot of numbers by zero," Josh answered. "We would have to try different numbers, too," added Allie.
>
> "Good, but what do you mean by different numbers, Allie?" Angela asked.
>
> "Like some even and some odd," Allie replied. "Some big and some small, too," added Joey.

Rather than using a random set of numbers, Allie and Joey wanted to select from different types of numbers. This is an important step toward trying to construct a more general argument because it does not depend on checking a random set of examples. The reasoning is that if a conjecture holds true for a particular type of number (for example, an even number), then it likely holds for all numbers of that type. In this sense, a number is used as a place holder or representative of a class of numbers and not for its specific numerical attributes.

THINK ABOUT IT 6.3

Think about a conjecture your students have made recently during math class. What type of argument did they develop to convince themselves, you, or their peers that their conjecture was true?

But children's arguments can—and should—extend beyond checking particular cases, even with well-chosen numbers. One way to do this is to encourage children to use previously established generalizations as the basis for their arguments. As noted earlier, June Soares' third graders constructed a more general argument when they reasoned that the sum of 3 odd numbers was odd because "2 odds make an even and when you add odd plus even, you get odd." That is, they invoked two previously established generalizations ("the sum of any 2 odds is always even" and "the sum of any odd and any even is always odd") to think about what would happen when any 3 odd numbers were added. They did *not*, however, use an empirical argument of testing sums of 3 particular odd numbers (for example, $1 + 5 + 7$).

In a similar manner, rather than look at examples of sums of 4 odd numbers, Laura Panell's fifth grader Gail reasoned that the sum of any 4 odd numbers would be even "because there are 4 numbers and that is an even amount of odd numbers so it's even" (see Chapter 2, page 17).

When children explore functional relationships, they sometimes test their conjectured relationship empirically by looking at specific cases of the function values. For example, with the Trapezoid Table Problem (see Figure 3–6, page 36), to convince themselves that the number of people who could be seated at t tables was $3t + 2$, June Soares' class "tried many examples from the chart and it worked all of the time. We even tried some big numbers like 100." In other words, once children had developed a function rule, they compared specific function values to the data in their table ("chart") to see if the rule held. So, if the pattern in the function table indicated that 8 people could be seated at 2 tables, they tested their conjectured relationship by substitution: because $3(2) + 2 = 8$ was true, the function was true for that particular example. Once they had tried "many examples," they were convinced that their function rule was accurate.

But in this task, children's reasoning did not end with testing examples. Some were able to argue more generally about the accuracy of their function by reasoning from the context or structure of the problem, using intrinsic features of the task to model the function[7] (this can be challenging for more complicated functions). By examining the configuration of the tables, children saw that there would always be one person on each end (2 total) and that each trapezoid table always had 3 people on both sides. Because the number of trapezoids varied, then the number of people who could be seated on the sides depended on this varying quantity and could

---

[7]Chapter 4, for example, illustrates how children might reason from the context of the Growing Snake Problem to develop a functional relationship.

be expressed as "3 times the number of tables," or $3t$. However, the number of people on the ends was always 2 and was always added to the number of people who could be seated on the sides. June wrote, "They realized the 3 came from the people who could sit "on the top and the bottom" and the 2 "came from the two sides."

When children's arguments involve reasoning from the context of a problem, they are connecting intrinsic features of the problem—such as the fact that one person would always be seated at each end of the table configuration—to a mathematical model. This type of justification is not only accessible for children in elementary grades, it also frees their thinking from the limitations of an empirical approach in which they test particular numbers.

With an empirical approach, we only know that the conjecture holds for the particular numbers tested. While this might convince children initially, you can help them begin to appreciate the limitations of this type of justification. With most conjectures, it is impossible to test all possible cases. As a result, there is always a degree of uncertainty about the truth of the conjecture. Help children begin to look for more general arguments by techniques such as reasoning from the problem context or using previously established generalizations. As you develop this sensitivity in children's thinking, their justifications will become more sophisticated over time.

TEACHER TASK 6.7

Develop a conjecture that you can use to help your students see the limitations of an empirical approach testing specific (numerical) cases or examples. (See Appendix B, page 193 for an explanation.)

While much more could be said about testing conjectures and the types of arguments children build, keep the following points in mind:

- Teach children to always test whether or not their conjectures are true. Give your students experiences with false conjectures. If appropriate, introduce the concept of a counterexample. Remember that a false conjecture can be an opportunity to create a new one!

- Questions such as Is this always true? and Will it always work? should be a common part of classroom conversations. Help children think about the domain or set of numbers for which a conjecture is true (or for which it is false).

■ Help children think about what it takes to convince someone that a conjecture is true or false. What is a good, convincing argument? Keep in mind that the answer to this will vary based on children's mathematical understanding.

■ Help children articulate their arguments clearly and compare them with their peers.

■ Help children move beyond empirical arguments that test particular cases or numbers to more general arguments, such as those based on reasoning with previously established generalizations or reasoning from the context of the problem.

■ Remember that a generalization is only as strong as the argument on which it is built.

Revise When children encounter a conjecture that is not true, encourage them to revise it to look for a true conjecture. Eventually, children will begin to do this on their own. For example, if they are looking for a functional relationship, they soon learn to revise a function until the relationship holds. Angela Gardiner's account of third graders solving Growing Caterpillar illustrates this (see Figure 6–15).[8] In this vignette, after Meg used data in the function table to show that Jak's conjectured relationship was false, the class worked to revise the function.

Generalize At this point, most of the work in building a generalization—exploring, conjecturing, testing, and revising—has been done. The final stage is to focus attention on what has been created (a generalization) and on its final form of expression, whether words or symbols. Children should view building a generalization as an important mathematical activity. It is at the heart of algebraic thinking. Show them you value their work—decorate your walls with the generalizations they build!

Building a Generalization: An Example Using Functions

Let's look again at the Trapezoid Table Problem (Figure 3–6, page 36). June described that her students first counted the number of people who could be seated at tables made of 1, 2, 3, and 4 trapezoid blocks and put these data

---

[8]See Chapter 3, page 52 for a complete account.

"Okay, what do you think the pattern is?" I asked. "I think it is
x times 2 plus one," Jak said. "How many of you agree with Jak?" I
questioned. "I don't know. I have to do a T-chart," explained Meg.
"Well, then let's do that together on the board," I said. With the
students' help, we drew the following T-chart on the board:

x	y
1	2
2	5
3	10
4	17

"Now that we have that on the board, I don't agree with Jak," said
Meg. . . . Because if it was x times 2 plus 1, then x would be 1 and y
would be 3. And, it's not. It's $x = 1$ and $y = 2$," she explained. The
class struggled with the pattern for a long time. "I see it, I know the
formula!" Joe cried out. "Well, what is it?" I prodded. "It's $x \times x +
1 = y$," he said.

Figure 6–15 *Children revise a function*

in function tables. Using the function tables, they found a recursive pattern
in the number of people ("add 3 to the number of people") and used this
to determine the number of people seated at 12 tables (see Figure 6–16).

What occurred next helped push children's algebraic thinking further.
June wrote:

Explore

I asked the class to look at the chart in another
way. I wanted them to look at the relationship
between the tables and the number of people.
Find the rule. No luck. I then gave them the
hint to see if there was a way to multiply and
then add some numbers to have it always work.
Jon suggested that we try and find a "secret
message."[9]

After a few minutes, believe it or not, Anthony
and Allison started to multiply the number of
tables with different numbers starting with one.

---

[9]*Secret message* was the term June's students coined to denote functions.

number of tables	number of people
1	5
2	8
3	11
4	14
.	.
.	.
.	.
12	38

$+3$

Figure 6–16 *Function table for the Trapezoid Table Problem*

Conjecture	The two children arrived at multiplying [the number of tables] by 3 and then they would have to add 2.
Test	We tried many examples from the chart and it worked all of the time. We even tried some big numbers like 100.
Generalize	We then tried to make a "secret message." Anthony said that the 3 stays the same so use a 't' for table. This is what he came up with:

$$3(t) + 2 = \text{number of people}^{10}$$

Test: Built justification based on problem structure	They realized the 3 came from the people that could sit "on the top and the bottom" and the 2 came from the 2 ends.

---

[10]Notationally, $3(t)$ is the same as $3t$ or $3 \times t$.

During this activity, June's students

■ *explored* how the two data sets were related by looking for patterns represented in the function table;

■ *conjectured* a relationship and described it in everyday language ("The two children arrived at multiplying [the number of tables] by 3 and then they would have to add 2"). Once they had tested their conjecture, they later described it more symbolically as "$3(t) + 2$ = number of people";

■ *tested* this conjecture by looking at specific cases; further justified their conjecture by reasoning about the physical problem and its relationship to the numbers in their function ("They realized the 3 came from the people that could sit 'on the top and the bottom' and the 2 came from the 2 ends.").

■ At the end of the task, they had built a *generalization* which they described in symbols as $3(t) + 2$ = number of people.

"Posing conjectures and trying to justify them is an expected part of students' mathematical activity" (NCTM 2000, 191).

Conclusion

As you begin to transform your practice, keep in mind that children's ability to reason algebraically builds over time. It is helpful to revisit ideas— or even tasks—throughout the school year. This allows children time to reflect on complex ideas and organize their thinking over time. Be flexible in your plans. If there's an opportunity to spontaneously change an arithmetic lesson (or conversation) into an algebraic thinking one, follow this.

Teaching practices that develop children's algebraic thinking call on a specific set of skills. This chapter described four important practices: (1) help children learn to use a variety of representations, to understand how these representations are connected, and to be systematic and organized when representing their ideas; (2) ask questions that challenge children to explain and compare their ideas, to build and justify conjectures about mathematical relationships and patterns, and express conjectures in increasingly sophisticated ways; (3) listen to children's thinking and use this to find ways to build more algebraic thinking into your instruction;

and (4) help children build generalizations through exploring, conjecturing, and testing mathematical relationships. Above all, note that these practices are centered on children. The goal is for teaching to focus on *children's* ideas, *their* reasoning, *their* representations, *their* conjectures, *their* arguments, *their* generalizations—in short, *their* algebraic thinking.

Changing *Where* I Teach

Algebraic thinking is not an add-on to your existing mathematics curriculum. But when you consider all the subjects you teach every day, along with testing and accountability pressures, or even professional development priorities adopted by your school and district, you might not feel reassured by this statement. Knowing how to find time for early algebra might seem challenging; however, as we will see in this section, elementary teachers are skilled at finding creative ways to get around these barriers. In particular, Chapter 7 includes insights from teachers' classrooms on how algebraic thinking can be integrated into areas such as literacy, science, social studies—even physical education. Chapter 8 describes some of the ways teachers have drawn other teachers, principals—and parents—into early algebra. The central theme of this section is that opportunities for early algebra are all around you—not just in the mathematics classroom!

CHAPTER 7

Algebraic Thinking Across the School Curriculum

So far, we've looked at *what* to teach and *how* to teach. Let's turn our attention to *where* to teach. Algebraic thinking is not just for the math classroom. In fact, doing the kinds of activity described in this book in classes other than those designated for math instruction gives children important experiences with seeing math in action and for building connections across domains of knowledge. This chapter draws on elementary teachers' classroom-tested ideas to think about ways you might integrate early algebra into the other subjects you teach. You will see how they have taken tasks described in this book—or created their own—to bring algebraic thinking into areas such as language arts, science, social studies, and even physical education. As you read this chapter, think about the subjects you are teaching and where there might be novel opportunities for early algebra.

Using the Telephone Problem to Link Language Arts, Social Studies, and Science[1]

When the Literacy Initiative at June Soares' school began to place significant demands on her classroom time, she started to look for creative ways to integrate algebraic thinking into other subjects in her third-grade classroom. The first three hours of the school day were designated for literacy instruction, so a natural starting point for her was to look for ideas in the books she had selected for read-alouds. Using these as a resource, she began

---

[1]See also Soares, Blanton, and Kaput (2005).

to design algebraic thinking tasks to go along with literacy instruction and soon found ways to link these tasks to other subjects.

One occasion was a social studies unit on immigration. For this unit, June used the story line from the book *How the Second Grade Got $8,205.50 to Visit the Statue of Liberty* (Zimelman 1992) and her adaptation of a problem from "All Lines Are Busy!" (Florence 2000) to create the Telephone Problem (see Figure 7–1). A variation of the Handshake Problem, the Telephone Problem (see Appendix A, page 183, for a solution) requires children to look for a relationship between the number of friends and the number of phone calls they make to each other, then use this relationship to predict how many calls there would be for 100 people.

But June extended this beyond literacy and social studies. Her class was also studying a unit on sound in science so, as part of this unit, they made telephones by attaching two paper cups with string. Children then used their paper telephones to act out the process of making phone calls for the Telephone Problem (see Figure 7–2). Talking to each other on the telephones they made during science class not only increased children's enthusiasm for the task, it also helped them see that it took two people to make one phone call.

Many children's books can be used to develop mathematical tasks that use algebraic thinking. You will find that some work better than others. Figure 7–3 summarizes some ideas for how you might incorporate early algebra into children's literature. Note that these suggestions do not

---

Telephone Problem

The second graders at the Jefferson School have raised money to visit the Statue of Liberty. Thirteen friends are planning to go. They are very excited about the trip and worried that they might forget something! On the night before the trip, they call each other to double-check what they need to bring. Each friend talks to every other friend once. How many phone calls will be made? How many calls could be made if 14 friends were planning to go? Fifteen friends?

- How did you get your answer? Try to show your solution on paper.
- Organize your data in a table. Do you see a pattern in the numbers?
- How many phone calls would be made if 100 friends were planning to go?
- How would you describe the relationship between the number of friends and the total number of telephone calls?

Figure 7–1 *Telephone Problem*

Figure 7–2 *Children act out making telephone calls*

Hints for Using Children's Books to Develop Algebraic Thinking Tasks

- Are there quantities that change over time or that can be varied, such as the number of shirts a person has, the number of students going on a field trip, or the number of animals riding a bus? For example, in stories about animals, you can explore the total number of legs, eyes, tails, and so forth, for a group of animals of any size by varying the number of animals in the group.
- Are there architectural features that can be used as a context for thinking about geometric shapes and properties?
- Are there objects (e.g., cookies) that can be shared among a group? Changing the number of people in the group can quickly lead to an opportunity for building patterns.
- Do characters in the storybook have (different) quantities of some item (e.g., money, candy)? Making a known quantity unknown (see Chapter 2) is a quick way to bring in algebraic thinking.
- Can the book and the associated early algebra task be incorporated into another subject, such as science or social studies? If so, then the benefit of integration is increased.

Figure 7–3 *Ideas for integrating early algebra into children's literature*

necessarily require elaborate planning and preparation. You can pose questions that build algebraic thinking informally as you talk with your students about a story and its characters.

> My favorite comment was when one child said, "Cool, I didn't know our reading book has math problems!" They have become so excited about math that during reading time there have been several requests to do math instead of or along with the stories we are reading.
>
> *Andrew Gentile, fourth-grade teacher*

Poetry and Algebraic Thinking

I firmly believe that integrating curriculum is a good way to get around the overwhelming amount of it we seem to be required to teach. I have been successful in combining my reading and writing programs, and saw many opportunities to integrate language arts and the content areas of social studies and science. Math, for me, has always been difficult to integrate. I typically presented it as a stand-alone topic, despite my reminders to my students that "we find math everywhere." The lesson I presented in which I integrated math and poetry was a breakthrough for me. Exposing my students to the idea of using math in the context of poetry drove home the point that math really is all around us.

Laura Hunt, third-grade teacher

Poetry has a natural rhythmic structure that Laura used to get children to think about patterns in numbers. She noticed that children had trouble knowing where to insert line breaks in their poems; their writings looked more like prose than poetry. So she designed a task in which students developed their own syllabic patterns and used these patterns to write poems. To get started, Laura read a haiku to her students and had them count the number of syllables in each line. Children saw that the syllabic pattern was 5–7–5. As Laura shared her own 8-line poem with students, they tracked the syllabic pattern through a function table (see Figure 7–4).

Children immediately noticed that the numbers were odd. Clara went one step further. She described the number of syllables as "2 times the line number plus 1." In doing so, she not only identified a functional relationship between the line number and corresponding number of syllables, she also made the important step of using natural language to describe an arbitrary odd number. This expression (which could also be described here as "2 times an integer plus 1") is a precursor to the symbolic form $2n + 1$, in

line	syllables
1	3
2	5
3	7
4	9
...	...

Figure 7–4 *Function table comparing the line number and number of syllables*

which *n* represents any integer. Expressing an odd number (or an even number) in symbolic form is critical in later grades as students develop more formal arguments about conjectures involving even and odd numbers. What is worth noting here is that Clara's insight occurred in a poetry lesson!

After Laura shared her poem, she instructed each student to create a number pattern to use for the first 4 lines of their 8-line poem. They could then reverse or repeat the pattern for the next 4 lines. She advised that each line be no more than 12 syllables. Children wrote their poems based on their own syllabic patterns, then partnered with each other to decipher the patterns. Two of the poems and their syllabic patterns are included here (see Figure 7–5).

The poetry task can be easily adapted to the ability of your students. For younger children, learning to organize the data in a function table and to identify recursive patterns might be sufficient. As children's understanding develops, you can introduce more complex patterns and think about how to express relationships between the number of lines and the number of syllables as Clara was able to do in the data from Laura's poem.

This lesson was valuable to my students on many levels. They had to struggle a bit to fit the poetry constraints they had imposed on themselves, and they were forced to revise their writing. On a mathematical level, the lesson allowed the children to create, manipulate, and apply mathematical patterns to a real problem in a context outside of

Pixie Wing by Abby Sylvia	line	syllables
A pixie wing gliding through my doorway as I	1	12
feel its sprinkling magic dust, shimmering	2	10
like stars and tickle my nose as	3	8
I wedge myself in bed.	4	6
The silent ripple of	5	6
a pixie wing swiveling in	6	8
the morning breeze's mystic light, is wind	7	10
surfing gracefully across the swivelly grass.	8	12

Trains by Jeremy Isaacs	line	syllables
Train	1	1
rolls down	2	2
through darkness.	3	3
Slow, gaining speed.	4	4
Slow through tunnel,	5	4
through puddles.	6	3
Stopping.	7	2
Halts.	8	1

Figure 7–5 *Children's poems and syllabic patterns from Laura's lesson*

math. Some of the children who are usually the least outspoken in math class were the most highly engaged in this activity. There was lots of calculation practice embedded in the lesson, and opportunity for debates about patterns and structure.

Laura Hunt, third-grade teacher

Speed Stacking in Gym Class

When fourth-grade teacher Andrew Gentile walked into his students' gym class, they were quite surprised. He heard one student say, "This is so weird—math in gym class!" Another child responded, "Yeah, but it is so fun!" Students were learning hand-eye coordination through a speed-stacking unit as part of their wellness/physical education curriculum (for more information on speed stacking, see www.speedstacks.com). Andrew had created a functional thinking task that would get students to look for relationships between the number of stacks and the total number of cups by examining growing patterns in various stacking routines.

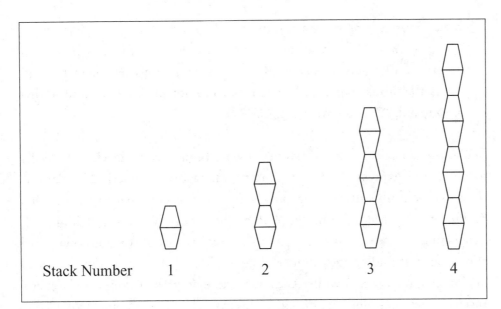

Figure 7–6 *Andrew's stacks of size 2, 4, 6, and 8*

He asked children to work in groups to form a growing pattern that followed a specific rule of their choosing. The instructions were fairly general because the class had already completed several functional thinking tasks. He demonstrated stacks of size 2, 4, 6, and 8 (see Figure 7–6), where the size of the stack referred to the number of cups being used. Children noticed that the stack number times 2 was equal to the number of cups in the stack, or stack size.

Following Andrew's example, one group created the simple linear relationship that they described as $S \times 3 = C$, where S represented the stack number and C represented the total number of cups. However, some children were able to create more complex relationships in how they stacked their cups. Andrew described one group's results:

The most interesting stack came from a group of 3 boys. They methodically organized four stacks of 4, 7, 12, and 19. I asked them how they were doing and they challenged me by saying, "I bet you don't know how many cups we will have in stack 5!" I . . . decided to get the class involved. One girl in my class . . . began to make a T-chart and told the class that the rule was plus 3, plus 5, plus 7, plus 9, etc. I agreed with her, but took this moment to review some of our other problems where they had to look left to right in the T-chart for a relationship. Two children recognized the function that they described as $N \times N + 3 = C$, where C represented the number of cups and N represented the stack number. Another group described this relationship as $S \times S + 3 = \text{cups}$, with *S* representing the stack number. Then something funny happened. The girls said, "I bet you guys don't know how many cups there will be in the 50th stack!" I was happy to see the boys tell them to hold on as they took paper and pencil and multiplied 50×50 and added 3 and said, "The answer is 2,503!"

Mathematically, Andrew's students were beginning to develop the skills to build and express their own linear and quadratic functional relationships symbolically, after doing only a few teacher-initiated tasks like this during the previous month. More than this, they were also beginning to understand the power of functions as a predictive tool for unknown situations, such as finding the number of cups for the 50th stack. But the focus of this chapter is that, while Andrew's students gained important experience in functional thinking, doing this in gym class in the context of a non-mathematical activity (speed stacking) helped shape their *mathematical* experience in important ways. As Andrew wrote:

> Everyone was amazed that we could do math in gym. . . . It was an eye-opener for students, the wellness teacher, and myself to do this activity. I think we all had a positive experience. The students realized that academic learning does not have to be confined to the four classroom walls. I learned that taking a risk such as this is definitely worth it.

The Candy Problem in Science Class

The Candy Problem (Chapter 2) is a simply worded task that challenges children to develop algebraic expressions comparing quantities that have unknown amounts. Since many of children's mathematical experiences are with *known* arithmetic quantities, a problem like this can reveal a lot about children's algebraic thinking and can provide you with a way to help children begin to symbolize unknowns. To give children more experience with this type of algebraic thinking in an integrated context, Lina Fidalgo created the task Onion Skin Cells (see Figure 7–7; see also Appendix A, page 178, for a solution), adapted from the Candy Problem, to use in her science class.

Like the Candy Problem, Onion Skin Cells gives children opportunity to express and compare unknown quantities. This new task, though, has an additional complexity because children can express Onion B in terms

---

Onion Skin Cells

We recently looked at onion skin cells under a microscope. All living things are made of cells. We observed that cells look like boxes and each box has a nucleus. Some pieces of onions had a lot of cells. Others had less. Consider the following information about Onions A, B, and C: Onion A has an unknown amount of cells. Onion B has 9 more cells than Onion A. Onion C has 4 less cells than onion A.

How would you describe the amount of cells each onion (A, B, C) has? Express your answer any way you can, using an inequality, a number sentence, a word sentence, pictures, tables, or charts.

Figure 7-7 *Onion Skin Cells Problem*

of Onion A or Onion C (similarly, Onion C can be expressed in terms of Onion A or Onion B). As Lina wrote, her students discussed these options:

Samantha made another T-chart and wrote Onion B and Onion C at the top of each column. Everyone seemed to think this was a good idea, but I had to ask her why she chose Onion B and Onion C as headers for her columns instead of using Onion A for one of the columns. She was quick to reply, "Because Onion C will have less than Onion B, so if we know Onion B then we already know Onion C." "Hmmm, I like the way you are thinking, but does Onion C have 4 less cells than Onion B?" I asked. "No" said Janson, "It has 4 less than A, not B." "Well, it is still less than Onion B." Samantha added. I liked where she was going with this so I asked her to explain what she meant. "Well, let's say that Onion A has 10 cells, Onion B has 10 + 9, which is 19, so Onion C has 10 − 4, which is 6. Onion C will always have the smallest number."

Although Samantha did not yet symbolize the relationship between Onions B and C, she was able to think algebraically about that relationship. That is, without knowing the value of Onion A (hence, Onions B and C), she could reason that if unknown C is less than unknown A and unknown A is less than unknown B, then unknown C is less than unknown B.[2] When she observed, "Onion C will always have the smallest number," she understood this relationship to be true *regardless of the particular number of cells for Onions A, B, or C*. That is, she knew the relationship held for all numbers.

---

[2]Mathematically, this is known as the transitive property of the inequality $<$.

Tasks that develop this type of (algebraic) reasoning in children's thinking build critical foundations for understanding higher mathematics. But, again, the point of this chapter is that these foundations can be developed outside of math class and through the use of simple tasks such as Onion Skin Cells.

TEACHER TASK 7.1

What concepts are you currently teaching in your science class? Are there any quantities that can be compared? Develop a task like the Candy Problem, in which unknown quantities can be compared. Give this to students as a Problem of the Week or Homework Challenge.

Crystals, Crabs, and Spaceships

This section provides other tasks, created by elementary teachers to use outside of math class, that you might use as a starting point for your own task designs. As you look at these, think about the concepts you are teaching in social studies, language arts, science, and so on. Where are there opportunities for children to think algebraically? Remember that even simple tasks can be engaging for students and can lead to rich classroom conversations that use algebraic thinking.

Growing Crystals

Lorraine Gagne designed the activity Growing Crystals (see Figure 7–8; see also Appendix A, page 171, for a solution) when her fourth graders began studying rocks and minerals in science class. Using this activity to complement children's science experiment with growing crystals gave them a way to extend their science investigations and mathematically model growth patterns in crystals.

Decorating Hermit Crabs

First-grade teacher Julie Boardman designed an activity based on the book *A House for Hermit Crab* (Carle 1987), which tells the story of a hermit crab that decorates its shell with things found in the sea. She designed the task Hermit Crab Decorates for her students (see Figure 7–9).

Growing Crystals

The fourth-grade class is growing crystals. After one day, their crystals looked like this:

After 2 days, their crystals looked like this:

After 3 days, their crystals looked like this:

Organize your data in a table. What will the crystals look like after 4 days? What relationship do you notice between the number of days the experiment has occurred and the number of crystals?

Describe this relationship in words and symbols.

Use this relationship to predict what your crystals will look like in 150 days, when school gets out for the summer.

Figure 7–8 *Growing Crystals*

Hermit Crab Decorates

In January Hermit Crab leaves his shell, and in February he finds a new one. In March he finds his first decoration, and in April he finds his second decoration. If he continues to find one new decoration each month, how many decorations will he have by August? September? October? Extra challenge: How many decorations will Hermit Crab have by the end of the year?

Figure 7–9 *Hermit Crab Decorates*

Figure 7–10 *A representation of how one first grader organized and recorded his data for Hermit Crab Decorates*

Julie's first graders used a variety of representations to model the task—pictures, function tables, even their own constructions showing a correspondence between decorations and months. For example, one child wrote the months of the year from left to right, with the number of decorations for a particular month beside that month (see Figure 7–10 for a similar representation).

After children had the opportunity to explore the task, Julie gathered them together for a discussion. She described their conversation:

> Through children's explanations I was able to elicit ideas for a class T-chart that went along with the story. I then asked the students what they noticed about the T-chart. Helen immediately said she saw a pattern. I asked her what the pattern was. She said, "It's one more each time." I said, "One more of what?" A bunch of students replied, "Decorations." So I said, "We can figure out how many decorations Hermit Crab will have as long as we know the pattern. I then asked, "How many decorations did Hermit Crab have in July?" Most students responded, "Five." I asked them, "What can we say about August?" James said, "There'll be one more. That would be six." I probed them a bit further by asking what the conjecture would be. I said, "What is going on in the pattern?" Most said, "One more each time." I said, "What is the conjecture here?" James replied, "You need to have one more each time to find out how many there will be for the next month." I told him that was a great conjecture. I finished up the lesson by reading the rest of the story aloud. The students were excited to find that their predictions came true!

It is important to keep in mind that children in first grade are learning different aspects of a functional thinking task than, say, a fourth grader might. For example, their focus might be on understanding different tools (such as function tables) for organizing their data, or connecting two quantities to each other (for example, month 3 corresponds to 1 shell decoration) and how to represent that relationship. Fourth graders, especially those who have had these types of experiences prior to fourth grade, are able to focus on more complex aspects of functional thinking, such as finding and symbolizing linear, quadratic, or even exponential relationships.

Algebraic Thinking on Mars

As part of her language arts instruction, fifth-grade teacher Robin Kolbeck designed a functional thinking task with a simple linear relationship for students to solve. After reading the book *Space Station Mars* (San Souci 2005) and discussing the story and new vocabulary terms, Robin gave students an activity that showed a growing pattern between the number of spaceships and the number of aliens on the spaceship (see Figure 7–11; see

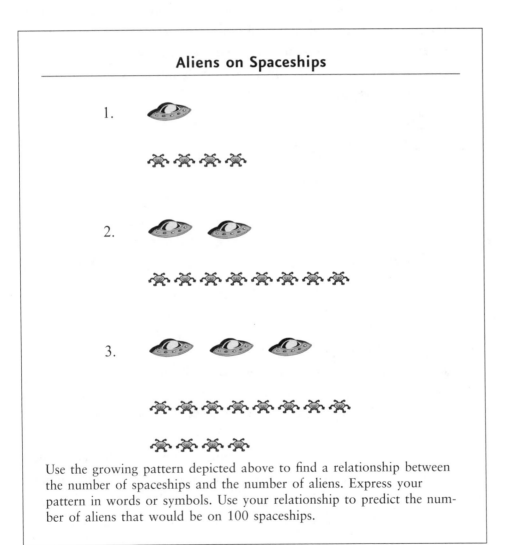

Aliens on Spaceships

1.

2.

3.

Use the growing pattern depicted above to find a relationship between the number of spaceships and the number of aliens. Express your pattern in words or symbols. Use your relationship to predict the number of aliens that would be on 100 spaceships.

Figure 7–11 *Growing pattern for the number of spaceships and aliens*

also Appendix A, page 160, for a solution). She then asked them to find a relationship between the number of spaceships and the number of aliens and use this to determine the number of aliens that would be on 100 spaceships (you might also use this task in science class). After students had completed this task, Robin asked them to work in pairs to design their own space problem.

Robin wrote about how students generalized the relationship:

Many of the students wanted to use multiplication for the answers. So then I asked them if they could come up with a conjecture or a way to solve for any amount of spaceships.

Angel came up with this statement, "As many spaceships as there are, multiply that number by 4 and you will get the amount of aliens there should be." She further symbolized this as $S \times 4 = A$, where S represented the number of spaceships and A represented the number of aliens. Many of the students used the T-chart to show the relationship between the amount of spaceships and aliens. I noticed that with only a few weeks of presenting this type of thinking, kids were starting to embrace and use it!

Hints for Getting Started

Oh, come on, can't we do one of those cool algebra tasks instead of reading?

Anthony, fourth grader

Hey, Mr. G, I made 10 algebra problems last night. Do you want to try them? Bet I can stump you!

Alana, fourth grader

This chapter illustrates some novel ideas and tasks elementary teachers have developed to expand children's access to algebraic thinking across the subjects they teach. Here are a few more ideas, contributed by teachers, that you might want to use as you integrate early algebra in your daily instruction.

Ask children to design their own algebraic thinking tasks. Have them share their tasks, and let the class solve them. Discuss how the tasks involve algebraic thinking. As teachers cited here found in their classrooms, this experience will give children a unique way to think about the mathematics of early algebra.

Think of ways to increase children's mathematical vocabulary. First-grade teacher Julie Boardman had an interesting approach:

> In our vocabulary lesson, I have a jar that says: Vocabulary Words Used in Daily Conversation. Every time someone uses a vocabulary word (new or old) in a sentence of conversation, I let that person put a cube in for the word used. This gets the students excited about using the vocabulary, and I've found that some of the words become so natural to them that they don't have the need to put a cube in. This is a good way to build children's vocabulary with words like *conjecture*, *pattern*, *relationship*, and *function*.

Encourage children to use math journals to reflect on their algebraic thinking. Third-grade teacher Laura Hunt wrote:

> Journals are a part of my everyday practice. My students write a lot through all areas of the curriculum, and we have a very rich writing workshop. In math class, however, journals were generally used to answer questions from our discussion book, or to solve daily math problems. They were pretty much filled with numbers, and I rarely looked at them. I guess you could have considered them scratch pads. Since I began integrating algebraic thinking, our math classes have become so vibrant with oral language. My students were wrestling with problems and discussing math concepts with one another. I decided to use [snack time] more efficiently by having students reflect in their math journal about our math lesson as they ate. I have been pleased to see responses that reveal understandings, misconceptions, and insights to group dynamics.

Conclusion

There are many ways to connect mathematics to other subjects and to provide children with wonderful opportunities to think algebraically outside of math class. Taking math lessons to a gym class, for example, helps children—and teachers—develop different ways of seeing and understanding mathematics. The activities in this chapter, if given during math instruction, would be a different experience for children. All you need to do is think beyond your designated math time and build an algebraic experience for children that will connect their learning in powerful, productive ways.

The following ideas summarize the key points in this chapter:

- Design tasks that can be used with read-alouds during language arts.

- Identify areas in different subjects where children might study quantities that grow (for example, populations in social studies, bacteria in science, cup formations in physical education). Design a task that helps children model simple mathematical growth.

- Look for ways to thread an idea across multiple subjects (for example, June connected the Telephone Problem to social studies, literacy, and science).

- Ask other teachers to assist you in implementing the activity (for example, Andrew worked with the physical education teacher for the speed-stacking activity).

- Ask children to design their own algebraic thinking tasks.

- As another way to connect literacy and mathematics, use math journals as tools for students to write about their generalizations and their arguments for why a conjecture is true or false.

Remember that your tasks do not have to be complicated, elaborate designs. Tasks as simple as Onion Skin Cells offer quick ways to get children thinking algebraically.

CHAPTER 8

Algebraic Thinking Across the School

Changing what you teach, how you teach, and where you teach might seem overwhelming if you are the only person in your school doing so. It helps to have at least one teacher to partner with, to share task ideas, children's thinking, and instructional successes and challenges. But the more your entire school is involved in early algebra, the better and more connected children's mathematical experience will be. Children need early algebra experiences across the grades in order for complex ideas to build over time.

This chapter offers ideas contributed by elementary teachers and gleaned from professional development for taking early algebra beyond your own classroom to involve teachers, administrators, and even parents. It provides you with practical ways to build a school culture of algebraic thinking as well as a road map for leading professional development in your school or district.

Getting the Whole School Involved

Engage Teachers in a Schoolwide Activity

When third-grade teachers Laura Hunt and Angela Gardiner took a graduate course on algebraic thinking, they began working together in their school to test and share their ideas. They were excited (and surprised) at what they observed their children doing and, as a result,

Schoolwide Handshake Problem

Big Idea

We thought we could do something a little fun to focus students' attention on math. We would like to show how one math problem could be solved in several different ways. We are hoping to display the results of the problem in an area where all students will have access to the data. Hopefully this will generate excitement and math discussion.

The Handshake Problem

How many handshakes would there be in a group of three if each person shook hands with every person in the group once? How many handshakes in a group of four? Group of five? Group of ten? Your whole class?

Here's What We Would Like from You

We would love it if each classroom could do this problem sometime in the next several days. All we need is the solution to how many handshakes in your class and some visual representations of how your students solved the problem (we would love to display these for all to see). Our expectations are that we will see several different ways to solve this problem based on your grade level. The key to this problem is to have children notice the patterns, and we hope that some will make generalizations from this problem. Our main goal is that you all have some fun while doing math!

Figure 8–1 *An invitation to participate in a schoolwide algebra activity*

wanted to share this with other teachers at their school. Laura describes their experience:

Angela and I had such success with the Handshake Problem in our own classrooms. We wanted to share the energy it had created for us with others. We decided to pose a challenge (see Figure 8–1) to the school and ask other teachers to get involved. When we first presented the idea at a staff meeting, it was not met with eager enthusiasm. We had the support of our administration, though, so we persisted. One of the kindergarten teachers approached me and asked how I might go about doing the problem at her grade level. We had a great discussion, and she seemed confident and ready to give the problem to her students.

We had two students announce the challenge over the intercom (see Figure 8–2). They said a little about how much fun they were having thinking about algebra, and recommended to other students that they look for patterns in solving the problem. Now all 624 kids were on board!

AGGIE: Hi! We are third graders here at DES. In math class we have been studying algebra.

JACOB: We think that algebra is pretty cool! We want to share one of the first problems that our teachers had our classes solve. It's the Handshake Problem, and everyone in the school is going to have an opportunity to participate.

AGGIE: Our teachers asked us how many handshakes there would be in our class if each person shook everyone's hand once. Now we want to know how many handshakes there would be in the whole school!

JACOB: In the upcoming days your teacher will talk about this problem and ask you to solve it. Our advice to you is look for patterns, think outside of the box, and have fun!

Figure 8–2 *Aggie and Jacob announce the schoolwide Handshake Problem*

The first person to put up students' work was a fourth-grade teacher. Her students modeled different ways to approach the problem, and she displayed their work on a big poster board. Here was a model for other teachers, but this time neither Angela nor I had created it. This was a step in the right direction! Other teachers began adding their students' work. The kindergarten teachers decided to devote a whole day to the Handshake Problem. They integrated a song that was part of their curriculum, and created a model out of Unifix cubes. We did end up gathering a lot of school energy for this project.

If teachers in your school are not familiar with algebraic thinking activities, getting their participation might take a little convincing on your part. Laura and Angela prepared a set of hints based on their experiences with the Handshake Problem (see Figure 8–3) and distributed this to teachers. Laura wrote:

I could see that teachers were having a difficult time solving the problem. We realized we had better get a "cheat sheet" ready. We received a lot of positive responses from teachers after this went into their mailboxes. Nearly all of the school participated in the project.

Help!!!
It's the Handshake Problem!!!

Thanks for agreeing to participate! Having wrestled with this one ourselves, we thought we should probably lend a little insight. We found it helpful to have the children break into small groups to model the problem physically. This way they can "feel" the structure of the solution. It is important that they recognize that each pair of people only shakes hands *once*. Therefore, simply doubling the number of people involved will not work. Organizing the data collected may reveal some patterns. Children may start by listing the handshake partners within a group. For example, a group of Sue, Laura, and Angela would result in 3 handshakes: Sue/Laura, Sue/Angela, Laura/Angela. But what if we add Lorrie to the group? There would be 6 handshakes: Sue/Laura, Sue/Angela, Sue/Lorrie, Laura/Angela, Laura/Lorrie, Angela/Lorrie.

Organized in a T-chart, it looks like this:

number of people (n)	handshakes (h)
1	0
2	1
3	3
4	6

At some point it helps if you reveal the structure of the pattern that develops. Try this:

number of people (n)	handshakes (h)
1	0
2	$0 + 1 = 1$
3	$0 + 1 + 2 = 3$
4	$0 + 1 + 2 + 3 = 6$

The key to this is every time you add a person to the group, you add one plus every consecutive number up to one less than the total number in the group. This is probably as far as most elementary grade children can be expected to go with this problem. In order to solve for the total number of handshakes in your class, someone will have to be quite industrious and continue this pattern to arrive at a solution. But we all know there are kids who will rise to the challenge and do this!

Lower grades: It would be great to simply see some mathematical thinking that leads to a solution for a small number in each group. Any visual representations you collect would be great. Perhaps teachers at this level could solve for the total number of handshakes for the class.

Upper grades: Some children may recognize a pattern that will lead to a broader generalization (a "formula") so that they could solve for any number of people in a group. If you multiply the number of people in the group by one less than the number in the group, then divide by two, you get the total number of handshakes.

$$\frac{n(n-1)}{2} = h$$

Whatever you do, we hope it generates some productive math conversations, and adds an element of fun to the subject!

Figure 8–3 *Hints for the Handshake Problem*

Math Night—Bringing Parents on Board

Laura and Angela found that their enthusiasm about early algebra did spread to other teachers. But they didn't stop with teachers. They knew that it was also important for parents to understand what their children were learning. Laura described their experience with Math Night:

We decided to organize a Math Night for our school. Our principal was happy to have any family night, so she gave us the go-ahead. Angela and I once again addressed all teachers at a staff meeting. We sent notices to families of all students in third through fifth grade, inviting them to Math Night. Now we were asking for teachers' help to facilitate the evening. We had asked families to RSVP for planning purposes. Over forty families said they would attend.

We organized the night into three stations with 5 tasks total and planned for each family to spend 25 minutes at each station. Angela and I decided to let the volunteer teachers facilitate the stations, and the two of us "floated" among them to troubleshoot any problems.

Math Night was a great success. We received very positive responses from parents. People asked for more take home packets I had put together and have suggested that we have more Math Nights in the future. It was well worth the effort!

Angela was equally enthusiastic about parents' response to Math Night:

I think the most rewarding part of Math Night was the parents and staff expressing how wonderful the night was. I had one parent say, "I know you have been working with Shane for a few months now doing this kind of math. I just needed to tell you that the way he needs to think about this math is carrying over into his everyday activities. He thinks about things, especially when we are woodworking together, that he never thought of before. You can see the wheels turning as he thinks. It is truly amazing. Thank you for making them think!"

Although children enjoy the Handshake Problem, you might want to begin with an easier task for your school, especially if you want to focus on the earlier elementary grades. Because of its simplicity, Counting Dog Eyes (Chapter 3) is easily adaptable to earlier grades. With the encouragement of her principal, first-grade teacher Gail Sowersby took this task to her colleagues to try as a whole-school (grades K–5) activity. All grades participated, and teachers displayed children's work throughout the school building. To celebrate their work, children took "gallery tours" around the school to look at what other students and classes had done. A local bakery even contributed cookies shaped like dog biscuits for students to eat during their tours!

Monthly Math

As a school leader for a districtwide literacy initiative, June Soares looked for ways to incorporate algebraic thinking into her school's literacy program (see also Chapter 7). Forging these connections not only found much needed instructional time for early algebra, it also helped make both literacy and algebraic thinking more relevant for teachers (and students).

As an outgrowth of this, June took a lead role in establishing Monthly Math, a school-based project in which teachers identified "back of the textbook" concepts that were often overlooked and created a set of activities—including some early algebra activities—in which the whole school could participate on a monthly basis. The result was a growing schoolwide appreciation for the more difficult kinds of mathematics students could do. As one teacher described, Monthly Math "united the school."

Math Buddy Project

Fourth-grade teacher Andrew Gentile extended his school's Book Buddy Project—in which his fourth graders read stories to first graders—to the Math Buddy Project. With Math Buddies, each fourth grader was paired with a first grade student to help solve the Candy Problem (see Chapter 2). Andrew's students had previously solved this task. As Andrew wrote, students in both grades were excited about the project:

> We had a meeting with our book buddies and explained that we would be math buddies for the day. This generated a great deal of excitement. The kids from my room were the facilitators of the problem and the other teacher and I did very little except circulate. My kids explained symbols and each student pair came up with their own symbols. Most kids chose letter symbols such as *J*, *M*, and *C* for John, Mary, and Candy. I was happy to see my class be patient and answer questions. They have also picked up on questioning and guiding techniques from class time and were able to give hints and clues without telling the answers.

While only two groups were able to come up with $M = J + 3$ as an expression for the amount of candy Mary had, this was still one of the most worthwhile projects I have implemented. I was happy to see the cooperative work and excitement of the other teacher, too. She has suggested further Math Buddies meetings, and I told her I have several tasks to use with the children. She now wishes to share some of the tasks with her first-grade team. They will make modifications for their grade level and work on them during math time.

Homework Club

At her school, fourth-grade teacher Lina Fidalgo leads a Homework Club that meets every Monday. Lina began giving students early algebra tasks after they had finished their homework and found that students were excited about solving these particular tasks and working together in small groups. She placed one of her own students in each of the groups because of her students' early algebra experiences.

If your school does not have a Homework Club, you might want to start one. If the club has a mix of grades, use this as an opportunity for students from different grades to work in small groups and to experience how different grades might solve a task. Older students can mentor younger ones, as they did in Lina's club (or in Andrew's Math Buddies Project). Not only will this be a good experience for students, it also provides you with a context for talking with other teachers—whose students might be in your club—about the algebraic thinking children are doing.

Summary of Ideas

There are many ways for you to introduce algebraic thinking into your school. As other teachers have done, you might begin by focusing on a particular task for your whole school to implement, a particular grade or set of grades, an after-school program, a student mentoring project, or your school's collective professional development time. Ideas and practical tips, some developed and tested by teachers, are summarized here:

■ Talk with your principal or other appropriate personnel (for example, math coach, curriculum coordinator) about what you want to do. They can provide critical support for your ideas.

■ If necessary, find another teacher (or two) you can partner with initially. They do not have to be from your grade level.

■ Give a schoolwide activity that all teachers and students can participate in. Prepare and distribute a set of hints about the successes and challenges you've had—what worked and what didn't work with a particular problem.

■ Make children's work and participation visible. Display students' work throughout the school corridors. Let children make announcements over the school's loudspeaker about the task. Arrange for classes to take gallery tours to look at other children's work.

■ Have a packet of information and materials ready to share with teachers once you've implemented a schoolwide activity. Include in this articles that will help teachers understand early algebra in practical ways.

■ Implement schoolwide activities on a regular basis, such as through Monthly Math programs.

■ Invite the principal to your class and let children do an algebraic thinking task with him or her. It is important for school administrators to know what kinds of math children need to learn and to see what classroom activity looks like when they're learning it.

■ Organize a Math Night to get parents involved. Have parents solve the tasks and get children to explain the solutions. Create a packet of information and activities for parents to take home.

■ Develop a Math Buddy mentoring program for students.

■ Start an after-school Homework Club for students (if your school doesn't already have one) and use algebraic thinking tasks as part of the content.

■ Look for ways to coordinate algebraic thinking with other professional development initiatives at your school. The professional development doesn't have to be math based. For example, if your school is focusing on literacy, design algebraic thinking tasks that can be integrated into literacy instruction.

■ If your school has standardized tests that include algebraic thinking tasks, make these tasks a part of your professional development. Teachers indicate it is helpful and productive to identify links between early algebra and high-stakes testing.

■ Offer teachers tasks that are designed specifically to integrate with other subjects, such as language arts, science, or social studies. By doing so, you can take advantage of teachers' particular subject-area strengths and interests.

A Road Map for Leading Professional Development at Your School

At our last professional development day, I told the other teachers that I have been doing algebra problems during my math workshop time. I told them the types of problems we did and how I have been implementing the problems in class. I told them it was a great way to get kids to look at numbers in different ways. I explained how it was more than algebra; it also helps kids practice basic arithmetic. I showed them samples of students' work. I even explained the importance of organizing data, finding a recursive pattern, and finding a function. I talked so confidently about algebra that the teachers were intrigued. For the first time in my life, I was a math teacher!

Lina Fidalgo, fourth-grade teacher

Some of the most persuasive leaders of professional development are elementary teachers who have seen in their own classrooms how algebraic thinking can deepen children's mathematical experience. Often, it seems, these teacher leaders do not describe mathematics as their primary interest or strength, yet they show tremendous creativity in helping their colleagues develop algebraic thinking in their classrooms. The point is that *you* can be a teacher leader of early algebra at your school. The remainder of this chapter outlines a road map to help you get started.

Solve, Adapt, Implement, Share

These activities at the beginning seemed like they were going to be hard to do, never mind creating my own. I've realized that they are a lot simpler to create and implement than I thought. I am really impressed with how these activities have shaped my way and my students' way of thinking algebraically. They have really opened my mind up about algebra and how, if we put it into a simple form, our students can do it!

Lisa Furtado, first-grade teacher

The research and professional development on which this book is based connects teachers' learning of mathematics to their own classroom teaching

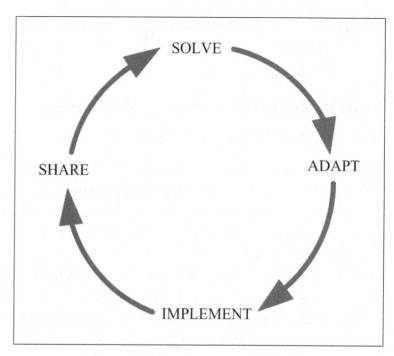

Figure 8–4 *Cycle of professional development*

experiences through a cycle of solving, adapting, implementing, and sharing early algebra tasks (see Figure 8–4). As Ma (1999) wrote, "Improving teachers' subject matter knowledge cannot be isolated from improving school mathematics teaching" (147). As teachers learn about building classrooms that foster children's algebraic thinking, they benefit greatly from the symbiosis in these steps.

Solve

It is important for teachers to be able to solve and discuss an early algebra task before using it in their classrooms. In many cases, the early algebra content will be less familiar to teachers than the arithmetic they typically teach, so understanding the mathematics is a first step. Moreover, solving these tasks collectively provides a way for teachers to share their mathematical understanding and develop confidence in that understanding.

When you meet with teachers, give them sufficient time to solve the task that they will use with their students. Construct teacher groups that represent a spectrum of grades, rather than grouping teachers from a particular grade. Teachers gain valuable insights about their own students' learning by understanding the progression of ideas in how students from other grades might solve the task and the difficulties it could pose.

Remember to model the instruction that you want teachers to practice with their students (see Chapter 6). Your role is to question and listen in order to help teachers express and justify their generalizations. Avoid telling teachers how to solve a particular task. Allow them to contribute their solutions and discuss differences among solutions. Draw attention to the different ways teachers model the problem and represent their thinking and discuss how children in various grades might do this. Discuss the different ways teachers represent their generalizations so that you can help them develop a symbolic, algebraic notation from their natural language expressions. Talk about how to nurture this language in children's thinking as well.

Adapt

Ultimately, what teachers do in their own classrooms will need to extend beyond the life of a particular professional development program. It is important for teachers to be able to pull early algebra ideas from their own resources and materials or spot algebra opportunities as they occur spontaneously in classroom conversations. As the *Professional Standards for Teaching Mathematics* notes, "textbooks can be useful resources for teachers, but teachers must also be free to adapt or depart from texts if students' ideas and conjectures are to help shape teachers' navigation of the content" (NCTM 1991, 32).

Provide teachers from across grade levels with the same activity, with the directions that they redesign it for their grade level. This is an important part of teachers' learning because it helps them think about task wording (How should the task be worded for a first grader versus a fourth grader?), task parameters (Are the numbers too big? Should children think about the number of dog eyes for 1,000 dogs or only 10 dogs?), the types of manipulatives that might be useful, and so forth. As teachers think about the needs of their learners and how this connects to task design, both their content knowledge and their instructional knowledge with respect to early algebra are strengthened.

Once teachers have had a few opportunities to adapt (and implement) the activities you bring to the professional development, ask them to find tasks or ideas from their own curriculum materials to bring to share with the teacher group. This process is an important part of teachers' growth because it helps develop their task autonomy (your professional development will eventually end!) and it helps sharpen their understanding of what counts as early algebra. Practically speaking, sharing teachers' ideas with other participants also provides teachers with additional resources and activities.

Implement

The third step in the cycle is implementation. It is important to design professional development that allows teachers to implement specific activities with their own students and share their findings with teachers *over an extended period of time.* Studies have shown that it is less effective to have short, concentrated periods of professional development (for example, a week in the summer) that do not allow teachers to connect their learning to their classroom practices over a sustained period (Garet et al. 2001). Also, while the time frame in which you sequence tasks depends on your own school's needs, one activity approximately every two weeks should be a reasonable pace. Spacing tasks (and meetings) too far apart can make it difficult to establish continuity. It is also important that all teachers implement the same activity (adapted to their grade level) so that they can have a common discussion about their classroom experiences in your meetings.

As teachers implement a task, ask them to focus on their own classroom practice and children's mathematical thinking. Let these core areas constitute the heart of your discussions when teachers share their classroom findings. Figure 8–5 provides some possible questions that teachers might focus on during implementation and that can help guide your discussion during the share. If feasible, ask teachers to write a reflection about their classroom experience.

Questions to Guide Teachers' Thinking

Your practice: What did you notice about your classroom practice? What kinds of questions did you ask? How did you adapt the problem for your grade? What tools or manipulatives did you find helpful for children in solving this problem? How did you support the development of children's expression of ideas from natural language to more symbolic, algebraic notation?

Your students' thinking: What did you notice about students' thinking? What strategies did they use? What representations did they use? How did they model the problem? Did they use words, symbols, or pictures? How did they express their generalizations? What kinds of questions did they have? What kinds of arguments did they build to convince you and their peers that their solution always worked? How certain were they that their solution would work?

Figure 8–5 *Questions to guide teachers' thinking during implementation*

> *Solve*—Give teachers the task to solve in small groups. Construct groups with teachers from different grades. Model instructional practice in which you question and listen, but allow teachers to find and discuss their own solutions.
>
> *Adapt*—Ask teachers to adapt the task to their grade level. Once they've had some experience with this, ask them to contribute their own tasks and ideas to the professional development.
>
> *Implement*—Ask teachers to try their (adapted) activity with their students. Encourage them to focus on children's mathematical thinking and the nature of their classroom practice.
>
> *Share*—Give teachers the opportunity to share findings from their classroom. Focus your discussions on children's mathematical thinking and how teachers' practice supported children's activity of generalizing.

Figure 8–6 *Components of the cycle of professional development*

Share

Once teachers have implemented an activity, they need the opportunity to share their findings with other teachers. As teachers make cross-grade comparisons, they will better understand trajectories in students' learning. For example, understanding how algebraic notation develops from first through third grades, or how the forms of justification first graders use might differ from those fifth graders would use, or how the manipulatives a second grader needs becomes unnecessary for fourth graders strengthens teachers' own content knowledge as well as their understanding of how the particular experiences they provide in their grades support learning in other grades. Moreover, as teachers hear what works (or does not work) in other classrooms, they can further refine their tasks and practice to reflect this. Figure 8–6 summarizes the key ideas in this cycle of activity.

Order of Tasks for Professional Development

As you design professional development for your school or district, another consideration is the order in which you introduce early algebra tasks. While there is not a prescribed order per se, there are some general guidelines that you might find useful.

Generalized Arithmetic or Functional Thinking?

This book focuses on two essential domains of early algebra: generalized arithmetic and functional thinking. As you organize the mathematical content for professional development, one approach is to use a mixture of tasks from each area. This provides teachers with a more comprehensive understanding of early algebra and the variety of ways they can integrate it into instruction.[1] Generalized arithmetic allows teachers to draw on their existing knowledge of arithmetic, and that familiarity can bridge their introduction to algebraic thinking. Moreover, interspersing generalized arithmetic with functional thinking allows teachers time to absorb the (perhaps) less familiar world of functions.

While, depending on the strengths of your teachers and curriculum, you might choose to focus on only one of these domains, keep in mind that they are not intended to be taught in the classroom in isolation. They are both part of early algebra. Thus, helping teachers learn to think flexibly with both domains in professional development can translate into more flexibility in their daily practice.

Getting Teachers' Attention

A great starting point is a task such as Understanding Equality (see Figure 8–7). Because this task is easy for teachers to solve, it allows them to focus instead on how *students* might solve it. Teachers often think their students will place the number 8 in the box and are surprised to uncover the misconceptions students have about = and the variety of answers they will select other than 8.

Ask teachers to give this task to their students *without any hints on how to solve it*. Teachers should question their students to determine the different solutions students found and the reasons for these solutions, then share that information with other teachers. Use this task at your first meeting, or put it in teachers' mailboxes beforehand so that you can discuss their findings at your first meeting.

$$9 \quad + \quad 3 \quad = \quad \square \quad + \quad 4$$

Figure 8–7 *Understanding Equality*

---

[1]Other research and professional development programs have focused exclusively on either generalized arithmetic or functional thinking with excellent results. How you approach this will be based on the particular needs in your school or district. Teachers can benefit from either approach.

Not only is this task a great opener, it also can be a starting point for discussions about generalized arithmetic as a form of early algebra discussed in Chapter 2. The advantage of beginning with generalized arithmetic is that it builds on teachers' understanding of and vast experience with arithmetic. Because of this, generalized arithmetic might provide a more comfortable starting point for teachers.

With generalized arithmetic, the order in which you introduce concepts in your classroom can be coordinated with the order of the arithmetic concepts you teach. (Functional thinking typically has a less visible role in the elementary grades curriculum, so there is more flexibility in how you place these tasks.) If you are introducing evens and odds, then tasks that allow children to generalize about evens and odds are important. If children are learning about operations, you will want to help them generalize important properties of these operations (for example, the Commutative Property of Addition). When = is introduced, missing number sentences that help children develop a relational view of equality are helpful.

Because your professional development will likely include teachers from various grades focusing on different arithmetic concepts, the tasks you choose might need to be adapted for these purposes. For example, if teachers in early elementary grades are focusing on the operations of addition and subtraction, they can explore properties of these operations (such as commutativity) or generalizations about sums or difference of evens and odds. For later elementary grades, teachers can use the same task templates, but change the operations to multiplication and division.

Introducing Functional Thinking

Our discussion in Chapter 4 regarding the order of functional thinking tasks in your own classroom instruction applies to professional development as well. When you introduce functional thinking, keep in mind the type of function a task elicits. A natural progression is to go from linear to quadratic to exponential functions. You might want to start with simple linear functions such as Counting Dog Eyes or the Trapezoid Table Problem. Tasks like the Handshake Problem have a quadratic relationship that is sometimes difficult for students to symbolize, although there are other interesting ways to generalize the relationships in these tasks by leaving quantities, such as sums of handshakes, in unexecuted form (see Chapter 4). While exponential functions are more challenging (and students will need experience with multiplication and multiplicative reasoning in order to describe these functional relationships), children in earlier elementary grades can focus on generating and organizing data and, in some cases, looking for recursive relationships with these tasks.

A Sequence of Tasks

To help you get started, Figure 8–8 provides one possible order for introducing tasks or concepts in teacher professional development. (See Appendix A for selected tasks and their solutions.) It combines both generalized arithmetic and functional thinking tasks, and sequences functional thinking tasks from simple to complex. As you plan your task sequence, make sure you also include opportunities for teachers to contribute their own task designs. Although the placement of teachers' own designs is flexible, ask teachers to begin identifying early algebra tasks in their own resources, designing their own tasks, and sharing these with other teachers as soon as possible. Involving teachers in task design not only develops their ownership in learning, but also strengthens their understanding of early algebra content.

Finally, remember to extend teachers' experience beyond the math classroom. Share—or ask teachers to design—activities that integrate early algebra into language arts, social studies, science, even physical or art education. Share your ideas or some of the ideas discussed in this chapter for getting your school or district involved. By doing so, not only will you help teachers channel their strengths and interests into early algebra learning, you will help them develop greater skill in finding creative ways for children to think algebraically.

- Understanding Equality
- Counting Dog Eyes
- Candy Problem
- Trapezoid Table Problem
- Cutting String
- The Outfit Problem
- Triangle Dot Problem
- Generalizing Properties of Arithmetic (design your own task)
- Squares and Vertices
- Handshake Problem
- Embedded Rectangles
- Generalizing About Evens and Odds (design your own task)
- Folding Paper

Figure 8–8 *One possible order for introducing tasks*

Keep in mind that teachers often appreciate a set of resources to get them started, so prepare a packet of materials to hand out. Over time, teachers can draw from these materials or add to them as they begin to contribute their own ideas.

Conclusion

This chapter identifies ways for you to get your whole school—or even your district—involved in early algebra. As you and the teachers you work with begin to implement the ideas in this book, you will start to see a transformation in your students' ability to think mathematically. Students will deeply impress you with the depth of their thinking and the enthusiasm they develop for mathematics through early algebra. As you watch this unfold in your classroom, it will change how you think about mathematics and how you teach mathematics.

The ideas, teacher reflections, classroom vignettes, and children's work discussed here offer concrete ways to change (or continue to change) what you teach, how you teach, and where you teach so that algebraic thinking becomes a central part of elementary school children's mathematical experiences.

Building a classroom that develops children's algebraic thinking begins with one math lesson. It is a process that evolves over time as your understanding of content, curriculum, and instruction changes and as your students' thinking grows in response to those changes.

In the daily life of your classroom, it involves designing instruction that helps children explore structure and relationships in mathematical ideas through avenues such as generalizing arithmetic concepts or thinking and reasoning about functional relationships. It involves questioning children, listening to their thinking, helping them represent their ideas in multiple ways, and teaching them how to build convincing arguments for their claims. It involves supporting children in developing ways of talking about mathematics that grow from their own natural language to more conventional symbolic forms. It is about building children's understanding of arithmetic skills and concepts by embedding these notions in tasks that are richer, more meaningful, more challenging—and algebraic. It is not about adding on to your curriculum, but rather, about extending and deepening what you currently teach so that children develop a mathematical understanding that can help them navigate the study of more formal mathematics in later grades.

It does not occur solvely in the mathematics classroom. It connects mathematical ideas—algebraic ideas—across the variety of subjects you teach—language arts, social students, science, and beyond. It is about collaborating with teachers and administrators to build a school culture of algebraic thinking so that what you do in your classroom is supported, sustainable, and viable.

Finally, building classrooms that develop children's algebraic thinking is about access to ideas. It is about equity. It is about all children having the opportunity to learn to think and reason mathematically. It is about altering children's perception of mathematics from an experience of failure to an endeavor that is attainable, doable, and exciting. It is about preparing children to be successful in a global economy for which mathematical thinking is the currency. And it begins with you.

Selected word problems and suggested solutions are included here in alphabetical order.

Aliens on Spaceships

1.

2.

3.

Use the growing pattern depicted above to find a relationship between the number of spaceships and the number of aliens. Express your pattern in words or symbols. Use your relationship to predict the number of aliens that would be on 100 spaceships.

Solution: From the growing pattern, we can construct the following table where s represents the number of spaceships and a represents the number of aliens:

s	a
1	4
2	8
3	12

The functional relationship between the quantities can be expressed in words as "the number of aliens is four times the number of spaceships" or in symbols as $a = 4s$. Using this relationship, there would be 400 aliens on 100 spaceships.

Candy Problem

John and Mary each have a box of candies. Their boxes contain the same number of candies. Mary has 3 additional candies in her hand. How would you describe the amount of candy they each have?

Solution: We don't know the specific amount of candies either John or Mary have. We do know that they each have a box with the (same) unknown amount of candies, and Mary has 3 more candies than John because of the 3 candies in her hand. Thus, if we let n denote the (unknown) amount of candies in each box, then John has n candies and Mary has $n + 3$. The choice of the letter n is arbitrary.

Adapted from Carraher, Schliemann, and Schwartz 2008.

Counting Dog Eyes

Suppose you were at a dog shelter and wanted to count all the dog eyes you saw. If there was one dog, how many eyes would there be? What if there were two dogs? Three dogs? One hundred dogs? Organize your information. Do you see a relationship between the number of dogs and the total number of eyes? How would you describe this relationship?

Counting Eyes and Tails

Suppose instead you wanted to find out how many eyes and tails there were all together. How many eyes and tails would there be for one dog? Two dogs? Three dogs? One hundred dogs? Organize your information. Do you see a relationship between the number of dogs and the total number of eyes? How would you describe this relationship?

Solution (Counting Dog Eyes): Let d represent the number of dogs and e the number of eyes. Then the relationship is $e = 2d$. Children might describe this in words as "the number of eyes is twice the number of dogs."

d	e
1	2
2	4
3	6
.	.
.	.
.	.
100	200

Solution (Counting Eyes and Tails): Let d represent the number of dogs and p the number of eyes and tails. Then the relationship is $p = 3d$. Children might describe this in words as "the number of eyes and tails is three times the number of dogs."

d	p
1	3
2	6
3	9
.	.
.	.
.	.
100	300

Cutting String

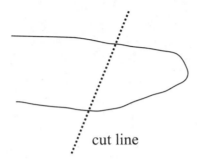

cut line

Fold a piece of string to make one loop. While it is folded, make 1 cut (see figure). How many pieces of string do you have? Fold another piece of string to make one loop. Make 2 cuts and find the number of pieces of string. Repeat for 3, 4, and 5 cuts.

How many pieces of string do you have for each number of cuts? Organize your data in a table.

What patterns do you notice in your data?

What can you say about the relationship between the number of cuts and the number of pieces of string? Write your conjecture in words or symbols.

Without cutting the string, use this relationship to predict the number of pieces that would result from 6 cuts. What about 100 cuts?

Solution: For 1 cut, there are 3 pieces of string. For 2 cuts, there are 5 pieces, for 3 cuts there are 7 pieces and so forth. If we let c represent the

(continued)

number of cuts and p the number of resulting pieces of string, we can organize these data as follows:

c	p
1	3
2	5
3	7
4	9
5	11

Note that data for the number of pieces, p, is a sequence of odd numbers. Reasoning from the context of the problem, we see that the first cut yields 3 pieces of string. Every time an additional cut is made, 2 additional pieces of string result. If we represent this as $2c$, then the number of pieces is $p = 2c + 1$. This might be expressed in words as "the number of pieces of string is twice the number of cuts plus the 1 end loop." Using this information, the number of pieces of string for 6 cuts would be $2 \times 6 + 1 = 13$, and for 100 cuts, $2 \times 100 + 1 = 201$.

Cutting a Two-Loop String

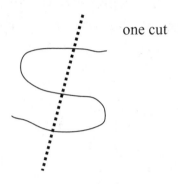

one cut

Fold a piece of string to make two loops. While it is folded, make 1 cut (see figure). How many pieces of string do you have? Fold another piece of string to make two loops. Make 2 cuts and find the number of pieces of string that results. Repeat this for 3, 4, and 5 cuts.

How many pieces of string do you have for each number of cuts? Organize your data in a table.

What patterns do you notice in your data?

What can you say about the relationship between the number of cuts and the number of pieces of string? Write your conjecture in words or symbols.

Without cutting the string, use this relationship to predict the number of pieces that would result from 6 cuts. Predict the number of pieces that would result from 100 cuts.

(continued)

Solution: One cut produces 4 pieces, 2 cuts produce 7 pieces, 3 cuts produce 10 pieces and so on. If c represents the number of cuts and p the number of pieces of string, we can organize the data in the following table:

c	p
1	4
2	7
3	10
4	13
5	16

The relationship between the numbers of cuts and pieces can be expressed in words as "the number of pieces is three times the number of cuts plus one," or $p = 3c + 1$. Using this relationship, we find that the number of pieces for 6 cuts is $3 \times 6 + 1$, or 19, and the number of pieces for 100 cuts is $3 \times 100 + 1$, or 301.

Embedded Rectangles

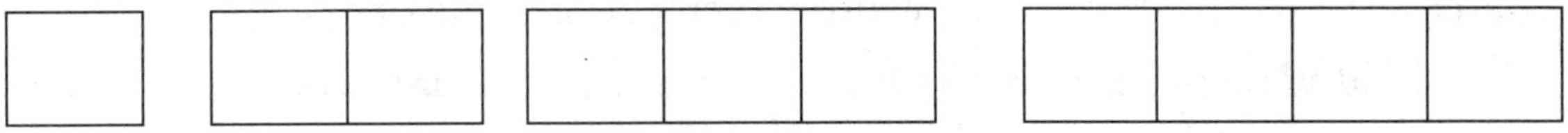

Figure 1   Figure 2   Figure 3   Figure 4

How many rectangles are there in Figure 1? Figure 2? Figure 3? Figure 4?

Do you see a pattern in your answers above? Describe it in words or symbols. How do you know it works?

Without drawing the next figures in the sequence, predict the number of rectangles in Figure 7. Test your prediction.

What can you say about the total number of rectangles in a figure of any size?

Solution: There is 1 rectangle in Figure 1. Disembedding the different rectangles in the remaining figures yields 3 rectangles in Figure 2, 6 rectangles in Figure 3, and 10 rectangles in Figure 4. You may recognize the similarity in these data to those in the Handshake Problem and the Telephone Problem. However, the data sets are not identical! There is a subtle difference (do you notice it?) that will yield a different functional relationship for the embedded rectangles task. Let f represent the figure number and r the number of rectangles. Then the functional relationship is $r = \frac{f(f + 1)}{2}$. Using this relationship, we find that there are $\frac{7 \times (7 + 1)}{2} = 28$ rectangles in Figure 7.

Folding Paper

Materials: One piece of plain white paper per student or group

1. Fold your paper in half. Open the paper and count how many regions this created on your piece of paper (see figure).

1 fold yields 2 regions

2. Refold the paper, then fold it in half again. How many regions do you now have on your piece of paper?

3. Fold the paper in half a third time. Count the number of regions you now have on your paper.

4. Organize your data in a table. Do you notice a relationship between the number of folds and the number of regions? How would you describe the pattern? Write it in words or symbols.

5. If you continued this process until you folded your original piece of paper 10 times, how many regions would this create? (Do not actually fold the paper to answer this.)

Solution: One fold yields 2 regions, 2 folds yield 4 regions, and 3 folds yield 8 regions. If we let f represent the number of folds and r the number of regions, we can organize these data in the following table:

f	r
1	2
2	4
3	8

Note that $2 = 2^1$, $4 = 2^2$, and $8 = 2^3$. In each case, the power of the exponent corresponds to the value of f. Generalizing this, we find that the relationship between the number of folds and number of regions is $r = 2^f$. Using this relationship, we find the number of regions for 10 folds to be $r = 2^{10}$.

Growing Caterpillar

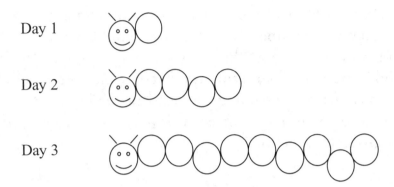

Day 1

Day 2

Day 3

A caterpillar grows according to the chart above. If this continues, how long will the caterpillar be on Day 4? Day 5? Day 100? Day *x*? (Measure length by number of circle body parts.)

Solution: Counting the head and body, on Day 1 the caterpillar measures 2 circles in length. On Day 2, it measures 5 circles and on Day 3, 10 circles. Using *x* to represent the number of days and *p* the number of body parts, we can organize this information as follows:

x	*p*
1	2
2	5
3	10

The functional relationship is $p = x \times x + 1$. We can use this to determine that the length of the caterpillar on Day 4 is $4 \times 4 + 1 = 17$ circles. On Day 5, its length is $5 \times 5 + 1 = 26$ circles, and on Day 100, $100 \times 100 + 1 = 10,001$ circles. (If your students understand exponential notation, you can express the relationship as $p = x^2 + 1$.) Another way to find this functional relationship is to reason from the

(continued)

context of the problem (see also Growing Snake). If you don't include the head in your count, then the number of body parts for each day is 1, 4, 9, and so on. You probably recognize these as square numbers: $1 = 1^2$, $4 = 2^2$, and $9 = 3^2$. The next number in the pattern would be 16, or 4^2. Since the day number is the same as the number being squared, for x days the number of body parts (not counting the head) would be x^2 circles. However, because we are including the head in the count, we need to add 1 to the number of body parts for each day ($1^2 + 1$, $2^2 + 1$, $3^2 + 1$, and so on). This gives the function $p = x^2 + 1$.

Growing Crystals

The fourth-grade class is growing crystals. After one day, their crystals looked like this:

After 2 days, their crystals looked like this:

After 3 days, their crystals looked like this:

Organize your data in a table. What will the crystals look like after 4 days? What relationship do you notice between the number of days the experiment has occurred and the number of crystals?

Describe this relationship in words and symbols.

Use this relationship to predict what your crystals will look like in 150 days, when school gets out for the summer.

(continued)

Solution: Let d represent days and c represent the number of crystals. On Day 1, there are 2 crystals, on Day 2 there are 4 crystals, and on Day 3 there are 6 crystals:

d	c
1	2
2	4
3	6

The number of crystals, c, is twice the number of days, d. We can express this relationship in symbols as $c = 2d$. Using this relationship, the number of crystals after 150 days will be $2 \times 150 = 300$.

Growing Snake

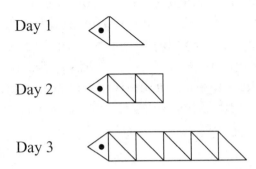

Day 1

Day 2

Day 3

A snake grows according to the chart above. If this continues, how long will the snake be on Day 10? Day *n*? (Measure length by number of triangle body parts.)

Solution: Counting the head and body, on Day 1 the snake measures 2 triangles in length. On Day 2, it measures 5 triangles and on Day 3, 10 triangles. Using *n* to represent the number of days and *p* the number of body parts (or triangles), we can organize this information as follows:

n	p
1	2
2	5
3	10

The functional relationship is $p = n \times n + 1$. We can use this to determine that the length of the snake on Day 10 is $10 \times 10 + 1 = 101$ triangles. (If your students understand exponential notation, you can express the relationship as $p = n^2 + 1$.) Another way to find this functional relationship is to reason from the context of the problem. If you don't include the head in your count, then the number of body parts for each day is 1, 4, 9, and so on. You probably recognize these as

(continued)

square numbers: $1 = 1^2$ (for Day 1), $4 = 2^2$ (for Day 2), and $9 = 3^2$ (for Day 3). The next number in the pattern would be 16, or 4^2 (for Day 4). Note that the day number is the same as the number being squared. Thus, for n days, the number of body parts (not counting the head) would be n^2. However, because we are including the head in the count, we need to add 1 to the number of body parts for each day ($1^2 + 1$, $2^2 + 1$, $3^2 + 1$, and so on). This gives the function $p = n^2 + 1$.

Handshake Problem

Arithmetic Task:
How many handshakes will there be if 3 people shake hands, where each person shakes the hand of every person once? How did you get your answer? Show your solution on paper.

Extension:
How many handshakes will there be if 4 people shake hands?
How many handshakes will there be if 5 people shake hands?
How many handshakes will there be if 6 people shake hands?

Organize your data in a table. Do you see a relationship in the numbers?

How many handshakes will there be if 50 people shake hands? How did you get your answer? What can you say about the relationship between the number of people in a group and the total number of handshakes? Describe the relationship in words or symbols.

Solution: If 3 people shake hands, there will be 3 handshakes. There will be 6 handshakes for 4 people, 10 handshakes for 5 people, and 15 handshakes for 6 people. If we let n represent the number of people and h the number of handshakes, we can organize these data in the following table:

n	h
1	0
2	1
3	3
4	6
5	10
6	15

The functional relationship between the number of people, p, and the number of handshakes, h, is $h = \dfrac{n(n-1)}{2}$. Using this relationship, the number of handshakes for 50 people is $\dfrac{50 \times (50-1)}{2}$, or 1,225 handshakes. (See Chapter 4, pages 58–64, for a more detailed discussion of the Handshake Problem.)

How Many Chickens?

Suppose Farmer Joe looks into his barn stall and counts 24 legs. He has 3 horses. If the remaining legs are on his prized chickens, how many chickens does he have?

Solution: Three horses have $3 \times 4 = 12$ legs total. This leaves $24 - 12 = 12$ legs, which must belong to the chickens. Since we don't know the number of chickens, we can represent this unknown quantity with a symbol. Let's represent it with c. Since each chicken has 2 legs, then 2 times the number of chickens yields 12 legs. That is, $2c = 12$. So, the number of chickens, c, must be 6, since 6 is the value that satisfies the equation $2c = 12$.

Outfit Problem

1. If you have 2 shirts and 3 pairs of pants, how many different outfits* can you make? Show how you got your solution.

2. How many outfits will there be if you have 3 shirts (and 3 pairs of pants)? What if you have 4 shirts? Five shirts? Organize your data in a table. Do you see a relationship? Describe it in words or symbols.

Based on your relationship, predict how many outfits there will be if you have 20 shirts (and 3 pairs of pants).

Ms. Sowersby's First-Grade Outfit Problem: If you have 1 shirt and 2 pairs of pants, how many outfits can you make? What if you have 2 shirts? Three shirts?

Assume an outfit consists of one shirt and one pair of pants.

Solution: You can make $2 \times 3 = 6$ outfits from 2 shirts and 3 pairs of pants. If you vary the number of shirts, you can make $3 \times 3 = 9$ outfits for 3 shirts, $4 \times 3 = 12$ outfits for 4 shirts, and $5 \times 3 = 15$ outfits for 5 shirts. Letting s represent the number of shirts and o the number of outfits, we can organize the data as follows:

s	o
2	6
3	9
4	12
5	15

The number of outfits will be the number of shirts times the number of pairs of pants (3). We can express this in symbols as $o = 3s$. So, for 20 shirts, you can make $3 \times 20 = 60$ outfits.

Onion Skin Cells

We recently looked at onion skin cells under a microscope. All living things are made of cells. We observed that cells look like boxes and each box has a nucleus. Some pieces of onions had a lot of cells. Others had less. Consider the following information about Onions A, B, and C:

Onion A has an unknown amount of cells. Onion B has 9 more cells than Onion A. Onion C has 4 less cells than onion A.

How would you describe the amount of cells each onion (A, B, C) has? Express your answer any way you can, using an inequality, a number sentence, a word sentence, pictures, tables, or charts.

Solution: Since Onion A has an unknown amount of skin cells, we can represent the amount as a. Since Onion B has 9 more cells than Onion A and Onion C has 4 less than Onion A, we can express the amount of cells in terms of a as follows:

Onion A has a skin cells
Onion B has $a + 9$ skin cells
Onion C has $a - 4$ skin cells

(Note that the amount of cells for each onion could be expressed in terms of Onions B or C as well. For example, if we let b represent the unknown amount of cells for Onion B, then the amount of cells for Onion A is $b - 9$, and the amount of cells for Onion C is $b - 13$.)

Saving for a Bicycle

Every week Mark's Dad gives him $3 for helping with chores around the house. Mark is saving his money to buy a bicycle. How much money has he saved after two weeks? Three weeks? Four weeks? How much money has he saved after twenty weeks? If the bike costs $60, how many weeks will it take to have enough money for the bicycle?

Solution: Mark has saved $6 after 2 weeks, $9 after 3 weeks and $12 after 4 weeks. After 20 weeks, he has $60 saved. It will take Mark 20 weeks to save enough money for the bicycle. After w weeks, he has saved $3 \times w$ (or $3w$) dollars. If we let A be the amount saved, then the functional relationship can be expressed $A = 3w$.

Spinner Problem

If you create a spinner by dividing a circle in half, what is the probability that the arrow will land on any one section of the circle? What if you divide the circle into thirds? Fourths? Fifths? If you divide the circle into n pie-shaped regions of equal size, what is the probability that the arrow will land on any one of the sections? (Assume outcomes are equally likely.)

Solution: For the first spinner, the probability of the arrow landing on a specific region is $\frac{1}{2}$. The probability is $\frac{1}{3}$ for the spinner with 3 sections, and $\frac{1}{4}$ for the spinner with 4 sections. For a spinner with n pie-shaped regions of equal size, the probability is $\frac{1}{n}$.

Squares and Vertices

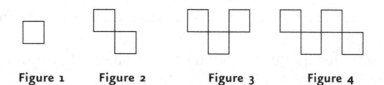

Figure 1   **Figure 2**   **Figure 3**   **Figure 4**

How many vertices are there in Figure 1? Figure 2? Figure 3? Figure 4?

Organize your information in a table. Do you notice a relationship between the number of vertices and the number of squares? Make a conjecture to describe the pattern you see. Use this to make a prediction about the number of vertices in a figure with 20 squares.

How many vertices would there be in a figure with *n* squares?

Adapted from NCTM 1997, *Mathematics Teaching in the Middle School, 4.*

Solution: Figure 1 has 4 vertices, Figure 2 has 7, Figure 3 has 10, and Figure 4 has 13. Using *s* to represent the number of squares and *v* the number of vertices, we can organize these data in a table as follows:

s	v
1	4
2	7
3	10
4	13

While there is a recursive pattern of "add 3" in the column representing the number of vertices, a functional relationship can be described as $v = 3s + 1$. If we use this relationship, then the number of vertices for 20 squares is $3 \times 20 + 1 = 61$. For *n* squares, the number of vertices is $v = 3n + 1$. We can also find the functional relationship by reasoning from the physical model provided. In Figure 2, the two squares each contribute 3 vertices plus the one vertex they have in common: $3 + 3 + 1$, or $3(2) + 1$.

(continued)

In Figure 3, counting left to right, the first two squares again each contribute 3 vertices plus the one vertex they have in common. For the third square, there are only 3 vertices remaining to contribute to the total. Counting these together gives $(3 + 3 + 1) + 3 = (3 + 3 + 3) + 1 = 3(3) + 1$ vertices for 3 squares. Similarly for Figure 4, we have the total from the previous count (in Figure 3), plus 3 remaining vertices from the last square in Figure 4. Counting these together gives $3(3) + 1 + 3 = 3(4) + 1$ vertices for 4 squares. For n squares, there are $3(n) + 1$ vertices. (Note that for Figure 1, there are 4 vertices, which can be expressed as $3(1) + 1$.)

Telephone Problem

The second graders at the Jefferson School have raised money to visit the Statue of Liberty. Thirteen friends are planning to go. They are very excited about the trip and worried that they might forget something! On the night before the trip, they call each other to double-check what they need to bring. Each friend talks to every other friend once. How many phone calls will be made? How many calls could be made if 14 friends were planning to go? Fifteen friends?

- How did you get your answer? Try to show your solution on paper.

- Organize your data in a table. Do you see a pattern in the numbers?

- How many phone calls would be made if 100 friends were planning to go?

- How would you describe the relationship between the number of friends and the total number of telephone calls?

Solution: This task is analogous to the Handshake Problem. In order to find the relationship, you might look at a more manageable number of friends first. For example, how many phone calls would there be if there were 2 friends? Three friends? Building from the Handshake Problem solution, if we let f represent the number of friends and t the number of telephone calls, then the total number of calls is $t = \dfrac{f(f-1)}{2}$. We can use this functional relationship to find the number of phone calls among 100 friends: $\dfrac{100 \times (100 - 1)}{2} = 4{,}950$.

Tower Problem

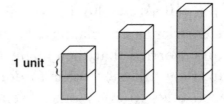

1 unit {

What is the surface area of each tower of cubes (include the bottom)? As the tower gets taller, how does the surface area change? What is the surface area of a tower with 50 cubes?

NCTM 2000. *Principles and Standards for Teaching Mathematics*, 160.

Solution: Surface area refers to the area of the outer surface of an object. The surface of a tower as pictured here consists of the combined areas of the top, bottom, and sides of the tower. For the smallest tower, the surface area is 1 square unit (top) + 1 square unit (bottom) + 8 square units (sides), or 10 square units total. Similarly, the second tower has a surface area of 14 square units, and the third tower has a surface area of 18 square units. The change in the surface area as the towers get taller can be described recursively as "add 4 square units to the surface area each time."

To find the surface area of a tower with 50 cubes, it is more efficient to find a functional relationship than to use a recursive pattern. Reasoning from the physical model, we see there will always be a contribution of 2 square units to the surface area based on the surface areas of the top and bottom of the tower. The quantity that varies is the surface area of the sides, and that variation is based on the number of cubes in the tower. For a tower of 1 cube (not pictured), the surface area of the sides is 4 square units, for 2 cubes the side surface area is 8 square units, and so forth. For n cubes, the surface area of the sides is $4n$ square units. Thus, for a tower of n cubes, the surface area, S, is $S = 4n + 2$. Using this, we find that the surface area of a tower of 50 cubes is $S = 4 \times 50 + 2 = 202$ square units.

Triangle Dot Problem

The figure below contains a drawing of a 5-dot triangle made by using 5 dots on each side. The 5-dot triangle requires a total of 12 dots to construct. How many dots will be used to make a 13-dot triangle?

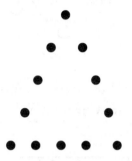

If *n* represents the number of dots on each side of an *n*-dot triangle, write an expression to represent the total number of dots in the triangle.

NCTM 1997, *Mathematics Teaching in the Middle School*, 2.

Solution: It might be helpful to look at cases for a 2-dot, 3-dot and 4-dot triangle. We find that a 2-dot triangle has 3 dots, a 3-dot triangle has 6 dots, and a 4-dot triangle has 9 dots. If you count the dots sequentially moving from one side to the next, you might notice that the total dots for the 2-dot triangle can be expressed as the sum $2 + 1$. For the 3-dot triangle, the sum can be expressed as $3 + 2 + 1$, and for the 4-dot triangle, the sum can be expressed as $4 + 3 + 2$. That is, the number of dots for a particular triangle can be found from the sum of three numbers: (the triangle dot number) plus (the triangle dot number $-$ 1) plus (the triangle dot number $-$ 2). (For the 2-dot triangle, the third addend is zero.) If we let *n* denote the triangle dot number and *d* the total number of dots, then we can express the relationship between the triangle dot number and the total number of dots in an *n*-dot triangle as $d = n + (n - 1) + (n - 2)$, or $d = 3n - 3$. (For an alternative way to think about this task, see the solution to Think About It 4.3, page 198, Appendix C.)

Trapezoid Table Problem

Suppose you could seat 5 people at a table shaped like a trapezoid.

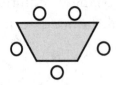

Figure 1

If you joined two trapezoid tables end to end (see figure 2) how many people could you seat at the new table? What if you joined 3 trapezoid tables end to end? Four tables?

Figure 2

Organize your data in a table. Can you find a relationship between the number of tables and the number of people seated? Use this relationship to predict the number of people that could be seated at 20 tables and 100 tables. Describe the number of people who could be seated at t tables.

How do you know your relationship works?

Solution: You can seat 8 people at 2 tables arranged as in Figure 2, 11 people at 3 tables, and 14 people at 4 tables. If we let t be the number of tables and p the number of people that can be seated, we can organize this in a table as follows:

t	p
1	5
2	8
3	11
4	14

Reasoning from the table design and seating arrangement, we see that regardless of the number of tables, each table would seat 3 people on the sides, not counting the ends (see Figure 3).

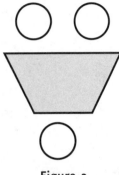

Figure 3

So, one table has 3 people seated on the sides, 2 tables have 6 people on the sides, 3 tables have 9 people on the sides, and *t* tables have 3 × *t* (or 3*t*) people seated on the sides. Also, there will always be 1 person seated on each end of the adjoined tables, contributing 2 additional people to the total amount of persons seated (see Figure 4).

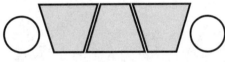

Figure 4

This reasoning leads to a function rule which might be described in natural language as "the number of people that can be seated is always 3 times the number of tables plus 2." You can write this symbolically as $p = 3t + 2$, where *p* represents the number of people and *t* the number of tables. Using this relationship, we find that the number of people who can be seated at 20 tables is 3 × 20 + 2, or 62, and at 100 tables is 3 × 100 + 2, or 302.

Answers to Selected Teacher Task Questions

Chapter 4

Teacher Task 4.1: Consider the following arithmetic question. How many rectangles are in the given figure?

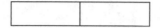

How can you transform this arithmetic task into one that involves functional thinking?

There are 3 rectangles in the given figure. (Disembedding a figure such as this into the number of distinct rectangles is an important geometric idea for children to consider.) For the associated functional thinking task and its solution, see Embedded Rectangles, page 167, in Appendix A.

Teacher Task 4.5: Once your students have completed Saving for a Bicycle, give them this modified task:

How would this relationship change if Mark had saved $5 before he began receiving an allowance?

If Mark had saved $5 before he began receiving an allowance of $3 per week, then he would have $5 + $3 = $8 after the first week, $5 + $6 = $11 after the second week, and so forth. Letting A represent the amount saved and w the number of weeks, the functional relationship would be $A = 3w + 5$.

Teacher Task 4.6: Find a functional relationship for Saving for a Bicycle if Mark receives an allowance of $4 per week. What if the allowance is $5 a week? How does the function change?

If Mark receives $4 per week, then he saves $4 after the first week, $8 after the second week, and so forth. Letting A represent the amount saved and w the number of weeks, the functional relationship is $A = 4w$. If his allowance is 5 per week, then the relationship between the amount saved and the number of weeks is $A = 5w$. The amount of money saved, A, is a multiple of the amount of money earned each week. The rate by which the amount saved, A, grows is equal to the amount earned each week.

Teacher Task 4.7: Construct the graphs of a linear function, a quadratic function, and an exponential function. For example, you might construct graphs of the functions from the Trapezoid Table Problem, Growing Caterpillar, and Folding Paper. How do their graphs compare? What do you notice about their similarities and differences? Find a recursive pattern in each function. Based on this pattern, what can you say about the rate at which each graph grows?

First, in order to compare the graphs of these functions, it is most helpful to graph them on the same coordinate axes:

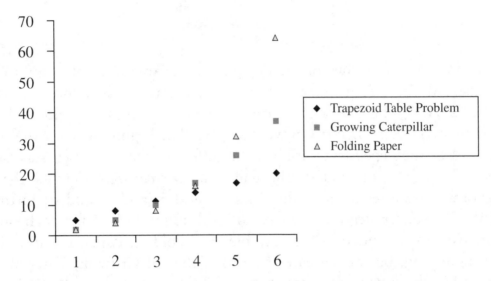

While there are similarities in the graphs (all three are increasing), there are noticeable differences in the rates at which they are growing. In particular, Folding Paper is ultimately growing the fastest, while the Trapezoid Table Problem has the slowest rate of growth. We can tell this visually by looking at the differences in the heights between points on the graph of a particular function and comparing these differences for the three different functions as the independent variable (on the horizontal axis) increases. For Trapezoid Table Problem, the height between any two points of data is 3 units. For Folding Paper and Growing Caterpillar, the difference between any two points is not constant. One way to see this is by identifying a recursive pattern in the data for each of the functions.

(continued)

Let's examine their function tables:

Trapezoid Table Problem			Growing Caterpillar			Folding Paper	
t	p		x	p		f	r
1	5		1	2		1	2
2	8		2	5		2	4
3	11		3	10		3	8
4	14		4	17		4	16
5	17		5	26		5	32
6	20		6	37		6	64

If we look at the values of the dependent variable (output column) for the Trapezoid Table Problem, the recursive pattern can be expressed as "add 3." That is, the difference between any two successive values of the dependent variable is 3. For Growing Caterpillar, beginning with the first two values of the dependent variable, the difference between two successive values is 3, 5, 7, 9, 11, and so on. This is an *increasing* difference that corresponds to the recursive pattern add 3, add 5, add 7, and so forth. In particular, the *difference* increases by an additional 2 units for each one-unit increase in the independent variable. For Folding Paper, the difference is also increasing, but at a greater rate than that of Growing Caterpillar. In particular, the difference amounts for Folding Paper are 2, 4, 8, 16, 32, and so on (as compared to 3, 5, 7, 9, 11 . . .). With Folding Paper, the difference increases by an increasing power of 2 rather than a constant 2 units. Note that between the third and the fourth function value, Folding Paper has a higher difference than Growing Caterpillar and this does not change. By comparison, both Folding Paper and Growing Caterpillar ultimately have larger growth rates than Trapezoid Table Problem, which has a constant growth rate of 3 units per unit change in the independent variable.

Chapter 6

Teacher Task 6.6: Depending on your grade level, have your students think about the set of numbers (for example, natural numbers, integers, fractions) for which the conjecture "multiplication makes bigger" is true and the set of numbers for which it is false.

With natural numbers, the multiplication of any numbers greater than one results in a product larger than either factor. For example, $3 \times 5 = 15$, which is larger than either 3 or 5. But $3 \times 1 = 3$, which is not larger than either 3 or 1. Thus, the conjecture is true for all natural numbers except 1 and 0.

If we extend this set to all fractions greater than 0 (note that natural numbers are also fractions for which the denominator is 1), then the result changes. If one of the factors in a product of two numbers is a fraction greater than 0 and less than 1 and the other factor is greater than or equal to 1, then the product will be *smaller* than the larger factor. For example, $\frac{1}{2} \times 4 = 2$, which is less than 4. If both factors are greater than 0 and less than 1, then their product will be less than either factor. For example, $\frac{1}{2} \times \frac{2}{3} = \frac{1}{3}$, which is less than both $\frac{1}{2}$ and $\frac{2}{3}$. For both of these cases, "multiplication makes smaller." However, if two factors are greater than 1, then their product will be larger than either factor. For example, $2\frac{2}{3} \times 4 = 10\frac{2}{3}$, which is greater than either $2\frac{2}{3}$ or 4. In this sense, "multiplication makes bigger." Thus, the claim that "multiplication makes bigger" is not always true.

Teacher Task 6.7: Develop a conjecture that you can use to help your students see the limitations of an empirical approach testing specific (numerical) cases or examples.

One approach is to develop a conjecture that is sometimes true and sometimes false. A possible conjecture is "an even number divided by an even number is always even." As shown in Think About It 6.2 (page 199), this is not always true. However, if children tested only cases where it was true (for example, $24 \div 4$, $16 \div 2$,

(continued)

36 ÷ 6, 12 ÷ 2), they might be convinced that it is true for all numbers. If children conclude that the conjecture is true based on testing specific cases such as these, then consider an example where the conjecture is false (for example, 12 ÷ 4). An example like this underscores the fact that testing cases can be misleading because what seems to be always true might not be.

Answers to Selected Think About It Questions

Chapter 2

Think About It 2.2: What other operations are commutative? That is, do numbers commute under subtraction, multiplication, or division?

Numbers do not commute under subtraction. For example, $3 - 4 \neq 4 - 3$. Numbers do not commute under division. For example, $3 \div 4 \neq 4 \div 3$. Multiplication is a commutative operation.

Chapter 3

Think About It 3.1: How would the function change if you used a different geometric figure (e.g., square, triangle, pentagon) with the condition that only one person could be seated on each side or end?

Suppose we change the Trapezoid Table Problem to one where the tables are squares and only one person can sit on each side or end. We would get the following data if tables were joined end to end:

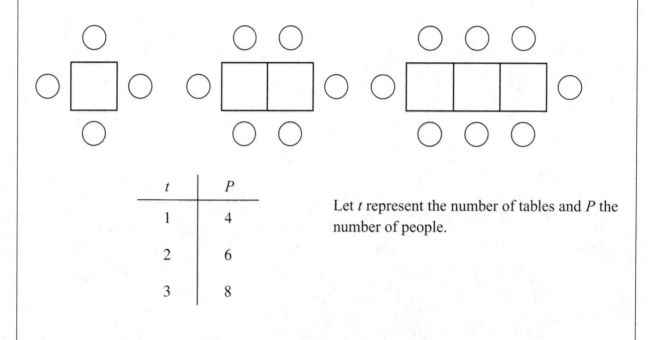

t	P
1	4
2	6
3	8

Let t represent the number of tables and P the number of people.

The new relationship would be $P = 2t + 2$ (the Trapezoid Table Problem had a relationship of $P = 3t + 2$). The difference in the functions is found in the number of people that can be seated on the sides (not ends) of each table. For square tables, 2 people can be seated on the sides for each table (thus, $P = \underline{2}t + 2$); for trapezoid tables, 3 people can be seated on the sides for each table (thus, $P = \underline{3}t + 2$). However, for each task the same number of people (2) can be seated on the ends regardless of the number of tables. Thus, $P = 2t + \underline{2}$ and $P = 3t + \underline{2}$.

If we change the Trapezoid Table Problem to one where the tables are equilateral triangles and only one person can sit on each side, we get the following data if tables are joined end to end (or, side to side in this case):

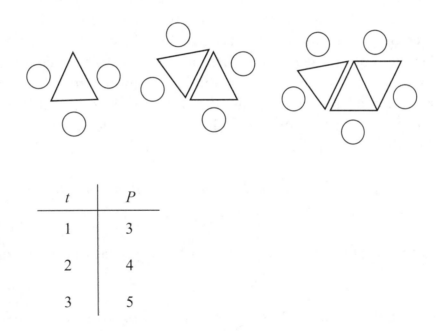

t	P
1	3
2	4
3	5

Again, letting t represent the number of tables and P the number of people, the functional relationship is given by $P = t + 2$.

Chapter 4

Think About It 4.3: It is important to remember that there are different ways to reason about and express solutions to a particular functional thinking task. Reasoning from the context (here, the physical model provided in Figure 4–6), can you think of another way to identify the functional relationship in the Triangle Dot Problem?

Another explanation is to note that each side of a triangle has n dots: A 3-dot triangle has 3 dots on each side, a 4-dot triangle has 4 dots on each side, and so on. Since there are 3 sides in a triangle and each side contributes n dots, then there are $3 \times n$, or $3n$, *nondistinct* dots. That is, the 3-dot triangle contains $3 + 3 + 3$, or $3(3)$, *nondistinct* dots, the 4-dot triangle contains $4 + 4 + 4$, or $4(3)$, *nondistinct* dots, and so on. However, if you think about how the dots are counted, you might observe that for each triangle, the vertices are always counted twice. The total number of (nondistinct) dots needs to be adjusted to account for this overlap. For the 3-dot triangle, since there are 3 vertices, each counted twice, we need to subtract 3 from the total number of (nondistinct) dots so that vertices are counted only once. Thus, the 3-dot triangle has $3(3) - 3 = 6$ dots. Similarly, the 4-dot triangle has $3(4) - 3 = 9$ dots, and so on. This suggests that the n-dot triangle has $3(n) - 3$, or $3n - 3$ dots.

Think About It 4.4: What might the Tower Problem look like if it did not involve functional thinking?

What is the surface area of the tower of cubes pictured here?

Think About It 4.5: What might the Spinner Problem look like if it did not involve functional thinking?

What is the probability that the arrow will land on one of the 3 regions? (Assume the circle is evenly divided into 3 regions and all outcomes are equally likely.)

Think About It 4.6: You should now have four different functions representing solutions to the tasks created by looking at cuts for 1 loop, 2 loops, 3 loops, and 4 loops. Do you notice any similarities or differences in the four functions? What changes? What stays the same? Can you describe a pattern in the form of the functions? What can you say about the functional relationship for a string that has n loops?

For 1-loop strings, the function describing the relationship between the number of cuts and the number of pieces is $p = 2c + 1$, where c is the number of cuts and p is the number of pieces. The function is $p = 3c + 1$ for 2-loop strings, $p = 4c + 1$ for 3-loop strings and $p = 5c + 1$ for 4-loop strings. The functions are all linear and all have +1 as part of the relationship. The part of the function that changes is the number by which c is multiplied. For 1-loop, c is multiplied by 2. For 2-loops, c is multiplied by 3. For 3-loops, c is multiplied by 4. In general, for each function, c is multiplied by a constant value equal to 1 plus the number of loops. Thus, the general form of the function is $p = (n + 1)c + 1$, where n is the number of loops in the string.

Chapter 6

Think About It 6.2: Consider the conjecture "an even number divided by an even number is even." Is it always true? Is it always false? What can you conclude about this? How would you revise the conjecture so that it is always true?

This conjecture is not always true. For example, $6 \div 2 = 3$, which is not even. But neither is the conjecture always false: $12 \div 2 = 6$, which is even. Sometimes it is true. Sometimes it is false. The question, then, is when is it always true? That is, for what numbers is an even number divided by an even number always even? Let's consider this conjecture in the context of even natural numbers (think about this question if the numbers are even integers, too). First, the divisor must divide the dividend with no remainder. Otherwise, the quotient is not a whole number and cannot be even. (For example, 4 and 16 are both even, but

(continued)

$4 \div 16$ is not a whole number and, thus, cannot be even. Or, 40 and 12 are even, but $40 \div 12$ is not a whole number.) Thus, the dividend must be a multiple of the divisor. Second, for the quotient to be even, the dividend must have *at least* one more factor of 2 than the divisor. For example, 24 has 3 factors of 2 and 4 has 2 factors of 2. That is, 24 has one more factor of 2 than 4. When 24 is divided by 4, the result is 6 (even). However, 8 and 24 each have 3 factors of 2 and $24 \div 8 = 3$, which is not even. (Think about the case when the dividend has fewer factors of 2 than the divisor.) So, when the dividend has at least one more factor of 2 than the divisor, the result is that not all factors of 2 are divided out of the dividend. At least one remains as a factor of the quotient. Thus, the quotient can be expressed as a multiple of 2 and will therefore always be even. (Note: If we said that the *only* condition was that the dividend must have at least one more factor of 2 than the divisor, then we can still get results that are not even. For example, 40 has 3 factors of 2 and 12 has 2 factors of 2. But, $40 \div 12$ is not an even number. Thus, we need the additional condition that the dividend be a multiple of the divisor so that the quotient is at least a whole number.)

Blanton, Maria, and James Kaput. 2003. "Developing Elementary Teachers' Algebra Eyes and Ears." *Teaching Children Mathematics,* 10 (2): 70–77.

———. 2004. "Design Principles for Instructional Contexts That Support Students' Transition from Arithmetic to Algebraic Reasoning: Elements of Task and Culture." In *Everyday Matters in Science and Mathematics,* ed. Ricardo Nemirovsky, Beth Warren, Ann S. Rosebery, and Jesse Solomon, 211–34. Mahwah, NJ: Lawrence Erlbaum Associates.

———. 2005a. "Characterizing a Classroom Practice That Promotes Algebraic Reasoning." *Journal for Research in Mathematics Education* 36 (5): 412–46.

———. 2005b. "Helping Elementary Teachers Build Mathematical Generality into Curriculum and Instruction," ed. Jinfa Cai and Eric Knuth, *Zentralblatt für Didaktik der Mathematik (International Reviews on Mathematical Education),* Special Edition on Algebraic Thinking 37 (1): 34–42.

Carle, Eric. 1987. *A House for Hermit Crab.* New York: Scholastic.

Carpenter, Thomas P., Megan Loef Franke, and Linda Levi. 2003. *Thinking Mathematically: Integrating Arithmetic and Algebra in Elementary School.* Portsmouth, NH: Heinemann.

Carraher, David, Analúcia D. Schliemann, and Judah Schwartz. 2008. "Early Algebra Is Not the Same as Algebra Early." In *Algebra in the Early Grades,* ed. James Kaput, David Carraher, and Maria Blanton, 235–72. Mahwah, NJ: Lawrence Erlbaum Associates/Taylor & Francis Group.

202

References

Dougherty, Barbara. 2008. "Measure Up: A Quantitative View of Early Algebra." In *Algebra in the Early Grades*, ed. James Kaput, David Carraher, and Maria Blanton. Mahwah, NJ: Lawrence Erlbaum Associates/Taylor & Francis Group.

Florence, Hope. 2000. "All Lines Are Busy!" *Mathematics Teaching in the Middle School* 5 (9): 600–02.

Garet, Michael S., Andrew C. Porter, Laura Desimone, Beatrice Birman, and Kwang Suk Yoon. 2001. "What Makes Professional Development Effective? Results from a National Sample of Teachers." *American Educational Research Journal* 38 (4): 915–45.

Hamming, Richard W. 1962. *Numerical Methods for Scientists and Engineers*. New York: McGraw-Hill.

Kaput, James. 2008. "What Is Algebra? What Is Algebraic Reasoning?" In *Algebra in the Early Grades*, ed. James Kaput, David Carraher, and Maria Blanton. Mahwah, NJ: Lawrence Erlbaum Associates/Taylor & Francis Group.

Kaput, James, and Maria Blanton. 2005. "Algebrafying the Elementary Mathematics Experience in a Teacher-Centered, Systemic Way." In *Understanding Mathematics and Science Matters*, ed. Thomas A. Romberg, Thomas P. Carpenter, and Fae Dremock. Mahwah, NJ: Lawrence Erlbaum Associates.

Kaput, James, David Carraher, and Maria Blanton, eds. 2008. *Algebra in the Early Grades*. Mahwah, NJ: Lawrence Erlbaum Associates/Taylor & Francis Group.

Kilpatrick, Jeremy, Jane Swafford, and Bradford Findell, eds. 2001. *Adding It Up: Helping Children Learn Mathematics*. Washington, DC: National Academy Press.

Ma, Liping. 1999. *Knowing and Teaching Elementary Mathematics*. Mahwah, NJ: Lawrence Erlbaum Associates.

Monk, Stephen. 2003. "Representation in School Mathematics: Learning to Graph and Graphing to Learn." In *A Research Companion to Principles and Standards for School Mathematics*, ed. Jeremy Kilpatrick, W. Gary Martin, and Deborah Schifter. Reston, VA: NCTM.

National Council of Teachers of Mathematics. 1991. *Professional Standards for Teaching Mathematics*. Reston, VA: NCTM.

———. 2000. *Principles and Standards for School Mathematics*. Reston, VA: NCTM.

San Souci, Daniel. 2005. *Space Station Mars*. Singapore: First Tricycle Press.

Schifter, Deborah. in press. Proof in the Elementary Grades. In *Teaching and Learning Proof Across the Grades,* ed. Despina Stylianou, Maria Blanton, and Eric Knuth. Mahwah, NJ: Taylor & Francis Group.

Smith, Erick. 2008. "Representational Thinking as a Framework for Introducing Functions in the Elementary Curriculum." In *Algebra in the Early Grades,* ed. James Kaput, David Carraher, and Maria Blanton. Mahwah, NJ: Lawrence Erlbaum Associates/Taylor & Francis Group.

Soares, June, Maria Blanton, and James Kaput. 2005. "Thinking Algebraically Across the Elementary School Curriculum," *Teaching Children Mathematics* 12 (5): 228–35.

Zimelman, Nathan. 1992. *How the Second Grade Got $8,205.50 to Visit the Statue of Liberty.* Morton Grove, IL: Albert Whitman.